LEVELS 3–4 ENGLISH

READING FOR UNDERSTANDING, ANALYSIS AND EVALUATION SKILLS

Jane Cooper

The Publishers would like to thank the following for permission to reproduce copyright material:

Photo credits Chapter opener image reproduced on pages **iv, 1, 17, 60** and **106** © Pressmaster – Shutterstock.

p.iv © dolgachov – 123RF; **p.v** © ONOKY/Alamy Stock Photo; **p.3** © dmussman – Fotolia; **p.11** © luchschen – 123RF; **p.23** © Danny Lawson/PA Archive/Press Association Images; **p.30** © aleksey ipatov – Fotolia; **p.32** © Pat on stock – Fotolia.com; **p.34** © Sapsiwai – Fotolia; **p.35** © Tan Kian Khoon – Fotolia; **p.38** (left) © Irina Tischenko – Fotolia; (middle) © vilainecrevette – Fotolia; (right) © alessandrozocc – Fotolia; **p.40** © Colorsport/REX/Shutterstock; **p.52** © Photodisc/Getty Images/ World Landmarks & Travel V60; **p.63** © Mirrorpix; **p.65** © veryolive – Fotolia; **p.67** © diego cervo – Fotolia; **p.70** © Andreas Stix – Fotolia; **p.74** © iwikoz6 – Fotolia; **p.77** © Andrew Milligan/PA Archive/Press Association Images; **p.83** © Vichaya Kiatying-Angsulee – 123RF; **p.97** © Wellcome Library, London (Copyrighted work available under Creative Commons Attribution only licence CC BY 4.0 http://creativecommons.org/licenses/by/4.0/); **p.98** © jeremy sutton-hibbert/Alamy Stock Photo; **p.100** © mihtiander – 123RF; **p.103** © Conrad Elias/Alamy Stock Photo

Acknowledgements See p.143

Every effort has been made to trace all copyright holders, but if any have been inadvertently overlooked the Publishers will be pleased to make the necessary arrangements at the first opportunity.

Although every effort has been made to ensure that website addresses are correct at time of going to press, Hodder Gibson cannot be held responsible for the content of any website mentioned in this book. It is sometimes possible to find a relocated web page by typing in the address of the home page for a website in the URL window of your browser.

Hachette UK's policy is to use papers that are natural, renewable and recyclable products and made from wood grown in sustainable forests. The logging and manufacturing processes are expected to conform to the environmental regulations of the country of origin.

Orders: please contact Bookpoint Ltd, 130 Park Drive, Milton Park, Abingdon, Oxon OX14 4SE. Telephone: (44) 01235 827720. Fax: (44) 01235 400454. Lines are open 9.00–5.00, Monday to Saturday, with a 24-hour message answering service. Visit our website at www.hoddereducation.co.uk. Hodder Gibson can be contacted direct on: Tel: 0141 333 4650; Fax: 0141 404 8188; email: hoddergibson@hodder.co.uk

First published in 2016 by
Hodder Gibson, an imprint of Hodder Education,
An Hachette UK Company
211 St Vincent Street
Glasgow G2 5QY

Impression number 5 4 3 2 1
Year 2020 2019 2018 2017 2016

Cover photo © Pressmaster – Shutterstock
Illustrations by Aptara Inc. (p.19, p.27, pp37–38, p.42 & p.50) and Peter Lubach
Typeset in Minion Regular 14/17 by Aptara Inc.
Printed in Spain

A catalogue record for this title is available from the British Library

ISBN: 978 1 4718 6860 3

CONTENTS

INTRODUCTION

This book is intended for those who are studying English at Levels 3 and 4. As well as broadening your reading skills, it will help to develop your understanding, analysis and evaluation skills.

Teachers should refer to Education Scotland's Literacy and English, experiences and outcomes document https://www.educationscotland.gov.uk/Images/literacy_english_experiences_outcomes_tcm4-539867.pdf for complete guidance and reference. However, the areas focused on in this book are:

	Third	Fourth
Understanding, analysing and evaluating – investigating and/or appreciating fiction and non-fiction texts with increasingly complex ideas, structures and specialist vocabulary for different purposes	To show my understanding across different areas of learning, I can: • identify and consider the purpose, main concerns or concepts and use supporting detail • make inferences from key statements • identify and discuss similarities and differences between different types of text. **LIT 3-16a**	To show my understanding across different areas of learning, I can: • clearly state the purpose, main concerns, concepts or arguments and use supporting detail • make inferences from key statements and state these accurately in my own words • compare and contrast different types of text **LIT 4-16a**
	To show my understanding, I can comment, with evidence, on the content and form of short and extended texts, and respond to literal, inferential and evaluative questions and other types of close reading tasks. **ENG 3-17a**	To show my understanding, I can give detailed, evaluative comments, with evidence, on the content and form of short and extended texts, and respond to different kinds of questions and other types of close reading tasks. **ENG 4-17a**
	To help me develop an informed view, I am exploring the techniques used to influence my opinion. I can recognise persuasion and assess the reliability of information and credibility and value of my sources. **LIT 3-18a**	To help me develop an informed view, I can recognise persuasion and bias, identify some of the techniques used to influence my opinion, and assess the reliability of information and credibility and value of my sources. **LIT 4-18a**

This book is divided into two main sections.

In Part One, there are two chapters about two of the key elements of the important skill of close reading:

- Chapter One will teach you about understanding writers' **ideas** and **details**.
- Chapter Two will teach you about how to examine writers' **language and style**.

In both chapters, there will be lots of examples for you to learn from, and lots of small tasks for you to do.

In Part Two, there is a series of practice assessments. Each one consists of a passage for you to read, and some questions for you to answer.

Your teacher might decide that you are going to work your way through the whole book, from the start to the end. But it is also possible to go straight to the second half of the book and use the practice assessments.

Texts

You will often hear your English teacher talking about **texts**. She or he might say, 'I want you to read all kinds of texts,' or 'We'll be looking at a new text today,' or 'When you get to fourth year you'll study a Scottish text for your exam.' She doesn't mean you'll be spending lots of English time with your phones out, texting each other!

When your English teacher talks about a text, he or she is talking about anything that is made out of language. A text is anything that can be used to communicate ideas, or experiences, or opinions, or information.

All of these things are texts:

- novels, short stories, plays and poems
- reference texts
- spoken words
- charts, maps, graphs and timetables
- adverts and promotional leaflets
- comics, newspapers, magazines
- CVs, letters, emails
- labels, signs, posters
- recipes, manuals, instructions
- reports
- reviews
- text messages, blogs, social networking sites
- web pages
- catalogues
- directories

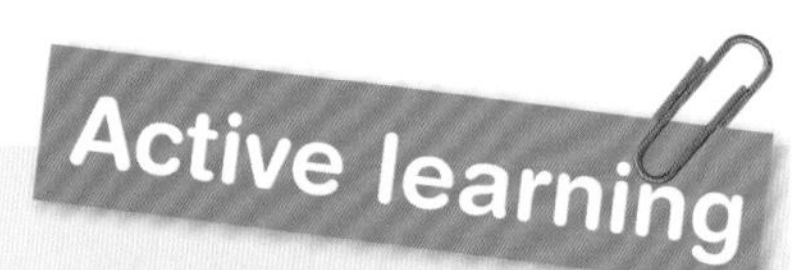

1 You have **5 minutes** for this first task. Look at the list of types of text in the blue box. How many of these can you find in the classroom?

2 You have **15 minutes** for this second task. Look at the list of types of text in the blue box. Now think only about the ones that you were not able to find in the classroom. How many of these do you think you would be able to find in other parts of your school? Where would they be? Your teacher might let you go off in pairs to find them.

3 You have **until your next English lesson** for this third task. Look at the list of types of text in the blue box. Now think only about the ones that you were not able to find either in the classroom, or anywhere else in your school. How many of these can you find outside of school and bring back to your next lesson?

So, as we have seen, the world is full of texts. People just never stop using language to communicate. Except when you are asleep, you are probably either making, or experiencing, texts every second of the day.

CHAPTER 1

Understanding Ideas and Details

Close reading

You will often hear your English teacher talking about the skill of **close reading.** In the National 5 and Higher exams this skill is called 'reading for understanding, analysis and evaluation'. Your parents might remember this skill being called 'comprehension' or 'interpretation' when they were at school.

Close reading is a good name for what you have to do – you have to be able to closely, carefully and thoroughly read all sorts of different texts. If you can read closely, you will be able to prove that you understand what texts say. You will also be able to analyse how writers put across their ideas, points and stories.

In this chapter we will mainly be looking at how you can prove that you **understand** the main ideas and the supporting details in a text. In close reading, the text is often called a **passage**, and we will use this term from now on.

One way to prove that you understand something is to be able to **explain** it to someone else.

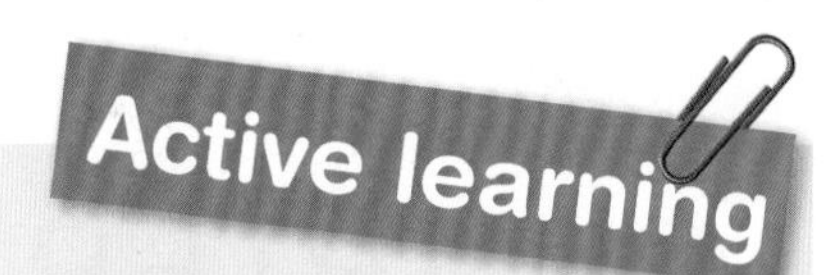

Think of something you understand. It could be:

- what makes your favourite team the best at their sport
- what makes your favourite band or performer the best
- how to cook or bake something, e.g. pancakes, a roast chicken, cupcakes, bacon and eggs...
- how to look after a particular animal, e.g. a dog, a cat, guinea pigs...
- how to get from your school to a particular other place, e.g. your home, the centre of your town, the nearest cinema...

or anything else that you can think of that you know you understand.

Now find a partner. Explain the information that you understand. You should try to talk for at least 1 minute but not more than 3 minutes. Then ask your partner to give you a mark out of 5 for how well you showed your understanding. Did you convince your partner that you understand this subject?

Using your own words

If you just repeat what someone says, or what somewhat writes, we will not know if you have really understood it. The most you can prove by repeating is that you have spotted the right section of the text to answer on, but you will not be showing that you **understand** it.

In close reading, the best way to prove that you **understand** one of the ideas or details that the writer is trying to put across is by being able to **explain** it. This usually means that you need to be able to put the writer's ideas into **your own words**. By using your own words, you are showing that your brain has processed the ideas and that you have really grasped them. We are going to work on that skill now.

Read this passage from a wildlife magazine:

> Angus is 8 months old. By the time he's 10, scientists predict that rhinos, African elephants and leatherback turtles will all be extinct in the wild. By the time he's 35, they predict up to 50 per cent of all bird species will be extinct.

A pupil read this and then put it into her own words. Here is what she wrote:

Angus is just a young baby. Experts forecast that, before his tenth birthday, it will only be possible to see rhinos, African elephants and leatherback turtles in zoos. They think that, when he reaches his mid-thirties, nearly half of all kinds of birds will have died out.

We can break this down to see how she put the original writer's ideas into her own words.

Original writer	Pupil's own words
Angus is 8 months old	Angus is just a young baby
By the time he's 10	before his tenth birthday
scientists predict	Experts forecast
extinct in the wild	a)
By the time he's 35	b)
up to 50 per cent	c)
all bird species	d)
will be extinct	e)

1 Three of the boxes on the right-hand side of the table have been filled in to show how the pupil put the original passage into her own words. The other five boxes have been left empty, except for the letters a) to e). Write these letters in your jotter. Beside them, write down the words of her own that the pupil used to show her understanding.

2 Some important words in the original passage have not been changed:

a) Which words were not changed?

b) Can you explain why the pupil chose not to change these words?

Here is the rest of the piece from the wildlife magazine:

> None of this has happened yet – and there's still time to stop it. If everyone who cares about nature takes as much action as they can, Angus might still inherit a world with wildlife, safe from the worst effects of climate change.

Copy and complete the table in your jotter to show how you would put these key sections into your own words.

Original writer	My own words
None of this has happened yet	
there's still time to stop it	
everyone who cares about nature	
takes as much action as they can	
Angus might still inherit a world with wildlife	
safe from the worst effects of climate change	

When we put something into our own words, we take the most important, useful words, the words that carry the meaning, and swap them for different words that have the same meaning. This is how we show our understanding.

So far we have worked on 'translating' a piece of text into our own words. However, you will never meet a close reading task that just tells you to put a chunk of the passage into your own words. Instead, you will be asked a question that tests your understanding of what the text says, and you will have to answer what the question asks.

Read this passage from the same nature magazine:

> I became very ill in 2015 and was bedridden for days on end. I realised I'd taken wildlife for granted. I was a busy working mum, so wrapped up in modern life that I never stopped to see the wonder of a sunset or notice the decline in our birds.

Suppose you were asked this question:

Explain the difficulty the writer faced in 2015.

The part of the passage you need to read to answer this question is:
'I became very ill in 2015 and was bedridden for days on end.'

You could answer the question in your own words by writing:

She became extremely sick and had to spend days at a time stuck in bed.

Now answer these two questions **in your own words**:

1. Give two reasons why the writer began to take wildlife for granted.
2. Explain two aspects of nature that the writer did not notice.

Below is another short passage. It comes from a book called *The Young Citizen's Passport*. The section you are going to read was printed inside the front cover.

Read the passage, and answer the questions that follow, using your own words as far as possible. The paragraphs have been numbered to help you.

The Young Citizen's Passport: your updated guide to the law

1 Whether you are at school, work, college or university, this book explains, as simply and clearly as possible, those parts of the law that have most relevance to everyday life.

2 We hope that you find the passport helpful.

3 Remember! In trying to summarise the law, we have had to leave out some details that may be relevant to your own situation. So don't rely on this book as proof of your legal rights. Always take further advice before taking any legal action. Often the best place to start is the Citizens Advice Bureau, but there are many others. Remember too that the law is always developing and changing.

4 The law is often a blunt instrument, and using it in the wrong ways can make matters worse. Try to sort things out personally, if you can. It's generally better to use the legal system only as a last resort, when everything else has failed.

→

1 Read paragraph 2. What do the writers of the passport hope?

2 Read paragraph 3.

a) Why have the writers had to leave out some details?

b) What do the writers say you should always do before taking legal action?

3 Read paragraph 4.

a) What **warning** do the writers give about taking legal action?

b) What **advice** do the writers give?

As you work through the rest of this chapter, remember that if you see the word '**explain**' in a question, that is a big hint that you need to use your own words in your answer. If the question asks you **how** something happens, then again you are being asked to explain, and should use your own words.

Giving evidence

We have just looked at knowing when you should answer in your own words, and how to do this. However, there are other times when you should do the opposite, and when you should use the words of the passage instead. That is what we are going to learn about now.

If you are ever asked a question where you need to give **evidence** from a text, you should do this by quoting. A **quotation** is a group of exact words taken from a text. If you use a writer's words as part of your answer, you are **quoting**.

Questions that ask you to quote can be worded in a number of ways. They might say:

- Quote the words that …
- Write down a word or phrase that shows …
- Which words show that …?
- What evidence is there that …?
- Which expression shows that …?

When you quote, you should put your answer inside quotation marks ('…') to show that you are using someone else's words and not your own.

Let us look at an example. First, read the passage below, in which TV presenter Miranda Krestovnikoff describes a memorable encounter.

I was filming for *The One Show* at Falmouth, from a shipwreck called *The Volnay*. The piece was going to be about life after a shipwreck – which creatures thrive once the boat goes down, and the food chain that is created. I'd got a beautiful pink sea fan as a prop – one of the new 'shipmates' on *The Volnay*. I was chatting away to the camera about the natural history of this species: they grow around a centimetre each year they're alive. This one was around 15 cm, which proved how long species can live with the right underwater environment. I started to hear some noise in my ear from the underwater communications team that were giving me my instructions, but I couldn't immediately make out what they were saying and couldn't see anything, so carried on with my lines, really fascinated with studying the fan closely.

It quickly became apparent that they were shouting, 'DOLPHIN! DOLPHIN!' really excitedly, and suddenly, right behind me, a bottlenose dolphin appeared. It was quite obvious it wanted to play and wouldn't leave me alone, I was blown away at how close it was, and with good visibility down deep that day I could see every detail. I have a strict rule of 'look but don't touch' when I'm in nature's home, but when a dolphin presents you with its belly and clearly wants it tickled, I don't think anyone would be able to resist.

Now look at the example questions and answers:

Q1 Which words in the first paragraph show that sea fans take a long time to grow?

A1 The writer says, 'they grow around a centimetre each year', which shows they grow very slowly.

Q2 What evidence is there in the first paragraph to prove that Krestovnikoff found the sea fan interesting?

A2 She says she was 'really fascinated with studying the fan closely', proving that she wanted to keep looking at it.

Q3 Which expression in the second paragraph explains why she could see the dolphin well?

A3 She writes that there was 'good visibility down deep that day', which made it easy for her to see the dolphin.

Did you notice that, in these answers, each quotation is still followed by a little bit of explanation? This proves that the person who wrote these answers has really understood them.

Now read the rest of the same passage, and answer the questions that follow. The paragraphs have been numbered to help you keep track.

1 I had a split second to decide whether to continue with the piece as planned, or to switch to talking about my sudden encounter. It was a pretty easy decision to be honest. We could revisit the original piece but we might never be this lucky again, not least because seeing a solitary dolphin is quite unusual – they are usually sociable creatures found in their pod.

2 The creature continued to circle me confidently, cheekily tipping over for a tickle and darting back and forth towards me. I'm sure if it could have spoken it would have said, 'Let's play!'

3 It was utterly magical.

4 After a while it was time to get out of the water and I really didn't want to. I had to do everything in my power to remain professional and start the ascent to the surface.

5 You can't engineer those kinds of interactions. The fact that this creature had found me, and stuck around for a playdate, was such an honour, and something I will probably never experience again.

6 He was a fickle chap. As soon as I'd come back up I saw him heading off to another small boat nearby, looking for his next playmate. But I'll never forget him; it was such a special, memorable experience and one that I'll never forget.

1 Quote the words in paragraph 1 that show the writer had very little time to decide what to do.

2 Write down a phrase from paragraph 1 that explains why it is unusual to see a dolphin alone.

3 Which two separate words in paragraph 2 show that the dolphin was not at all shy?

4 Which expression in paragraph 4 shows that the writer found it very hard to end her dive?

5 What evidence is there in paragraph 5 to prove that the writer thought this experience was really special?

You will get more opportunities to use the skill of quoting in evidence later in this chapter.

Understanding the writer's main ideas

So far, our questions have focused on either using your own words, or quoting in evidence, to show your understanding of some quite exact and narrow details. But if you truly understand what a writer is saying, you will be able to step back a little and explain the main ideas that run through a whole text or passage.

Read this advice and information for young people about banks:

> There are many reasons why it is a good idea to open a bank account. Firstly, most employers will not pay their staff personally or in cash, but only via a bank account. If you go to college or university and want to take out a student loan, this must also be paid into a bank account. Any money you keep in cash will always stay at the same value, but if you put it in a bank you will gain interest on your savings. You will also be able to pay bills simply straight from your bank account. Finally, the younger you are when you open one, the more you build up a credit history so that people can see a record of how you have looked after your money responsibly.

The main idea of this passage is that **it is a good idea to open a bank account**. You can show your understanding of this main idea by bullet pointing – in your own words as much as possible – the smaller details in the text that back up that idea. The result would look like this:

Why you should open a bank account

- Many employers will pay wages only into an account.
- An account is needed for a student loan.
- The money can earn interest.
- It provides an easy way to pay bills.
- It helps you build up a banking history.

Read the passage below about how to choose the bank that is right for you.

> There are many different banks to choose from. Thinking about the following things will help you decide which bank to open your account with. Is the bank easy to access: is there a branch near where you live or work, and can you get access to your account outside opening hours by using online banking or a mobile app? Does the bank have a good network of cash machines so that you can easily withdraw money when you need it? Will they pay you a reasonable amount of interest on any money you save in your account? How much will the bank charge you for its services? Do they have any special offers aimed at customers your age?

Now do these tasks:

1. Decide what the title should be for your bullet-pointed list. (Look back at the title in the example above if that helps.) Write the title in capitals in your jotter.
2. Now, using your own words as much as you possibly can, write a bulleted list of the important things a young person should think through before opening a bank account. **CLUE**: you should have five.

This skill of picking out the ideas running through a text or passage is a useful one. If you sit National 5 or Higher, you will find questions that ask you to do this in the exam called *Reading for Understanding, Analysis and Evaluation.*

Topic sentences

A topic sentence is a sentence, usually at the start of a paragraph, that tells the reader what a paragraph will be about. The sentence tells you the topic – the subject – of the paragraph. The rest of the paragraph should follow on from and build upon the idea that was introduced in the topic sentence.

Look again at this paragraph you have seen before:

There are many reasons why it is a good idea to open a bank account. Firstly, most employers will not pay their staff personally or in cash, but only via a bank account. If you go to college or university and want to take out a student loan, this must also be paid into a bank account. Any money you keep in cash will always stay at the same value, but if you put it in a bank you will gain interest on your savings. You will also be able to pay bills simply straight from your bank account. Finally, the younger you are when you open one, the more you build up a credit history so that people can see a record of how you have looked after your money responsibly.

The topic sentence has been picked out in bold type. It introduces what the rest of the paragraph is about. It says there are 'many reasons' for having a bank account, and the rest of the paragraph goes on and gives those reasons.

Now re-read this paragraph, which you have also seen before. Can you spot the topic sentence? **CLUE**: this time it is **not** the very first sentence.

There are many different banks to choose from. Thinking about the following things will help you decide which bank to open your account with. Is the bank easy to access: is there a branch near where you live or work, and can you get access to your account outside opening hours by using online banking or a mobile app? Does the bank have a good network of cash machines so that you can easily withdraw money when you need it? Will they pay you a reasonable amount of interest on any money you save in your account? How much will the bank charge you for its services? Do they have any special offers aimed at customers your age?

Sometimes, the topic sentence can come at the end of a paragraph, and work as a kind of summing up. Read this paragraph. The topic sentence has been picked out in bold.

> We had to get up at 5 a.m. and leave the ruined cottage without having any breakfast or a hot shower. The walk to the next village took eight hours, over steep and rocky mountain paths. Though it rained constantly, there was nowhere for us to shelter from the weather. Most of us got blisters on our feet, and as there were no rivers or streams to refill our water bottles from, we were soon very thirsty. **All in all, it was a really tough day.**

Remember: topic sentences give us the main idea of a paragraph. The rest of the paragraph builds up that idea by using supporting details.

Read the paragraphs below from a booklet about bullying. For each paragraph, find the topic sentence.

1. Everyone will deal with bullying differently. Some people can bounce back and recover. For other people the feelings are harder to deal with. Some victims of bullying become withdrawn and afraid. Some bullying victims may even go on and become bullies themselves.
2. There are good ways to cope with bullying. Talking to friends and family will help. So will doing the things you love, such as listening to music, playing games, or taking part in sport. These are all positive things that you can do to help yourself. They will not make the bullying stop, but they will help you to manage your feelings. Just being listened to can help you to feel more supported and less alone.
3. There are also some not so good ways to deal with being bullied. Arguing, taking out your anger on others, or missing school may seem like ways to cope, but they are not healthy. They will not deal with the bullying, or with how it makes you feel, and they will do you more damage in the long run.

4 You might find it very helpful to talk to a friend about what is happening. Your guidance teacher at school can also be very supportive. If you go to a church or mosque, perhaps a leader or youth worker there will be able to support you. If you don't feel comfortable talking to someone that you know, you can phone an advice service like ChildLine (0800 1111). In fact, there are lots of people around who can help you if you are being bullied.

Now you are going to try writing some paragraphs of your own that build on a topic sentence.

Task 1

Pick one of these openings. Write it down as your topic sentence. Add at least four more sentences to create a paragraph:

- There are lots of interesting things you can do on a boring Tuesday evening.
- There are lots of interesting things you can do at the weekend.
- There are lots of interesting things you can do in Glasgow/Edinburgh/London/Florida/Spain.
  (Pick one, or choose another place name you could write about.)
- There are lots of interesting things you can do during the summer holidays.
- There are lots of interesting things you can do with a loaf of bread.

Task 2

Pick one of these sentences to use as a topic sentence at the **end** of your paragraph. Write at least four more sentences to create a paragraph that builds up to that topic sentence.

- In fact, she had always hated Santa Claus.
- Altogether, it was a really wonderful day.
- It turned out to be his best birthday ever.

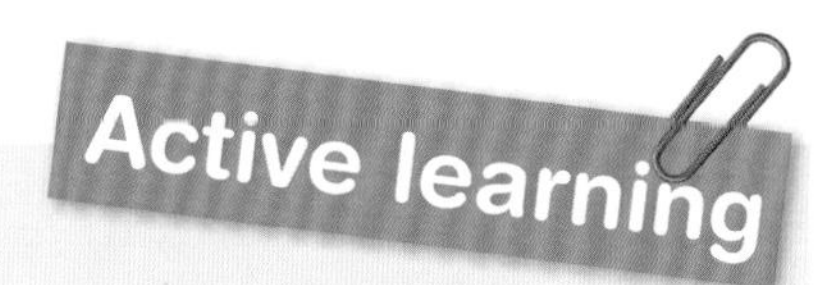

Bringing it all together

In this chapter you have learned when to use your own words, and when you should quote. You have also looked at how to prove that you understand a writer's ideas. It is time to bring these skills together in one task.

Read the passage about healthy eating, which came from a website.

1 Children who eat a balanced diet in the morning and during the day are in far better shape mentally and physically to get the most out of school.

2 **Breakfast** An extra 10 minutes in bed is NOT going to stand you or your kids in better stead than something decent to eat at the beginning of the day. If time is tight, try just a banana and a small yoghurt to provide energy and a good mix of nutrients – even whizzed into a smoothie if that's the deal-breaker with your child! Ideal breakfasts include oats and protein dishes like eggs. Make sure you're not skipping breakfast whilst running around after everyone else. You'll feel better for eating and you'll be setting a good example for your children.

3 **School lunches – a hot and healthy meal** School lunches have many benefits. Getting your children to eat school lunches will save you time, as there's no need to shoehorn food prep into your morning routine. They are also healthy: school lunches have to be nutritionally balanced to provide a wide range of vitamins and minerals and a limited amount of saturated fats, salt and so on. Homemade packed lunches rarely have such high nutritional value. If your children will be going straight from lessons to after school clubs and activities, it's good to know they ate well at lunchtime. Studies also show that at key times like starting in a new class or school, children prefer school lunches because they can be part of a group activity and make friends. These meals can even make children more adventurous. If your child sees friends eating chili con carne or fish pie they are much more likely to give it a go themselves. Packing them off with the same cheese sandwich every day doesn't encourage a well-rounded eater.

4 **Packed lunches – a homemade healthy alternative** The advantage of giving your child a packed lunch is that you know what they're eating. If you include food you know your child enjoys you'll avoid hungry days if there

isn't anything on the school lunch menu he or she likes. Packed lunches can help you save money too. School dinners are costed to be as affordable as possible, but at secondary school children can often buy their own combinations, and the cost soon adds up. Avoid giving them pre-packed snacks and drinks and you will save even more money. Bringing lunch from home also cuts out waiting. School canteens often have long queues but packed lunch eaters can sit down straight away.

5 If you are making packed lunches, try to keep them varied, nutritious and fresh. Try carrot and cucumber sticks in a pot if your child gets bored with apples, and a thermos flask of soup or even pasta instead of sandwiches five days a week. Proteins help keep your child feeling full for longer and have a slower sugar release than carbs – try egg, tuna, lean ham, cheese or chicken.

6 **After school** Older children and those who eat dinner late with the family will need something to keep them going after school. Make sure there's always a bowl of fruit out and encourage kids to snack on this whenever they like. Other things that will keep them going without too many 'empty calories' include wholemeal pitta and hummus, and yoghurt.

7 **In the evening** A substantial meal in the evening is a good idea because you don't know how much your child ate of his or her lunch when they were eating at school. Younger children should eat by 6 p.m. so their body has time to digest the food before bedtime. Even picky kids can enjoy hearty food.

8 **Pass it on – good brain food** Carbohydrates are the brain's favourite fuel – bread, cereals (not sugared), pasta, couscous, rice, root vegetables and things like baked beans. Vitamin C – which can be found in citrus fruits, strawberries, sweet peppers and leafy greens – boosts the brain's ability to learn.

First, answer the following questions about the writer's use of topic sentences.

1 Identify the topic sentence in paragraph 3.

2 Identify the topic sentence in paragraph 5.

Now you are going to answer a series of questions to show your understanding of the text above. The questions go in order throughout the passage, and the marks are an indication of how much information you need to give.

3 **Read paragraph 1. In your own words**, explain why children should eat a balanced diet. **2**

4 **Read paragraph 2.**

a) Which words show that the writer understands that parents are often in a hurry in the morning? **1**

b) Which word shows that a breakfast with oats or protein is the best kind? **1**

5 **Read paragraph 3.** The writer says that school lunches 'have many benefits'. **Using your own words as far as possible**, list the main benefits of these lunches. **5**

6 **Read paragraph 4. Using your own words as far as possible**, list the reasons why packed lunches can be a good option. **4**

7 **Read paragraph 5.** Explain two ways parents can make packed lunches varied. **2**

8 **Read paragraph 7.**

a) Which two separate words used in this paragraph both show that an evening meal should make people feel full? **2**

b) Explain why younger children should eat early in the evening. **2**

9 **Read paragraph 8.** Which expression shows that parents should share this healthy eating information with others? **1**

Summing up

In this chapter you have learned how to show your understanding of writers' ideas. You have been taught when you should use your own words, and when you should quote to give evidence. You have learned about topic sentences.

Close reading tasks usually do more than ask you to prove you understand **what** a writer is saying. You will usually be asked questions about **how** writers write, about their language and style. You will learn about this in the next chapter.

CHAPTER 2
Analysing Language and Style

How writers write

So far, you have learned about **what** writers write about, their **ideas** and **details**.

In this chapter we will be thinking about another aspect of writing, about **how** writers write. We call this aspect the writer's **style**.

Style is made up of the words, and the language techniques, that a writer chooses to use. As you work through this chapter you will learn, one by one, about some of these key techniques, and about the effects writers can create by using them.

Wonderful words

Vivid, varied vocabulary

Did you know that there are over 171,000 words in the English language? That is more words than in most other languages. Experts think this probably happened because English has borrowed from, and been influenced by, so many other languages. We have taken lots of words from the languages of other countries that have invaded Britain in the past. We have also taken words from countries that we have ruled, or traded with.

Some of our words come from Greek:

Some of our words come from the Vikings:

Some of our words come from the Saxons:

Some of our words come from languages spoken in India, which was ruled by Britain until 1947:

Look back at the groups of words above from the Greeks, the Vikings, the Saxons and from India.

- For each group of words, try to create a sentence that uses as many words as possible from that language, but still makes sense. You should end up with four sentences.
- Read over your sentences. Mark the best one with a star [*].
- Read out your best sentence to the class, and listen while everyone else in the class does the same with theirs.

After the Norman invasion in 1066 we got lots of words from French. For example, our words for farm animals come from Old English, but the words for the meat that we get from these animals come from French.

New words are still being added to English all the time, often to let us talk about new ideas and new ways of behaving. In the few years before this book was written, words like 'selfie', 'cake pop', 'e-cigarette', 'webisode', 'jeggings', 'onesie' and 'smartphone' were all added to English. By the time you read this book, we might even have decided that we do not need to use some of those words any more.

This all means that people who speak English can use a huge **vocabulary**, an enormous list of words that they know and understand. If you speak and write English, you just have a lot more words to play with. For example, in English we have two different verbs, 'make' and 'do'. These are some of the most common words in our language. But in German there is one shared word (*machen*) and in Polish (*robić*) for the idea of making and the idea of doing.

Because English has such a huge vocabulary, the language writers use can be very expressive and very varied.

First, read these three poems by pupils who were asked to write about a monster. Then do the tasks below.

First he chomped ten thousand drains
Then he munched some candy canes
Next he ate a giant cake
Last he drank a chocolate lake

First he ate a farm of tractors
Then he gulped a cast of actors
Next he scoffed the whole of Mars
Last he drank in fifty bars

First he ate a field of sheep
Then he swallowed a big fat neep
Next he gulped a squirming weasel
Last he drank a tank of diesel

1 These pupils were trying to use varied and interesting vocabulary to put across the idea of the monster eating. Sometimes the pupils just used the basic words 'ate' and 'drank'. But there are five more expressive eating and drinking words. Write them down in your jotter.

2 How many more expressive and interesting words can you think of for the actions of eating and drinking? Spend 3 minutes writing a list of these words in your jotter. Then compare your list with the words other people in your class thought of.

3 Now, try your own poem. Use the structure below. Be as imaginative and descriptive as you can about what the monster ate and drank. Remember to use varied and expressive vocabulary.

First he _____

Then he _____

Next he _____

Last he _____

There are lots of other areas where English has many different words for us to choose from. For example, let us think about how we go somewhere on our feet. The simplest, most basic word we have for that action is 'walk'. This word tells us that someone goes somewhere by putting one foot in front of the other, again and again, until they end up where they want to be.

But there are lots of other verbs we can also use to talk about someone going somewhere by putting one foot in front of the other. If we just think about the ones that start with the letter **s** we can come up with:

stroll	stagger	strut
stride	saunter	stumble

Let us check that you understand what all those different words mean. You will need six volunteers from your class. Each volunteer should walk down your classroom in one of the ways above: one person should stroll, one should stride, one should stagger, and so on.

How many more expressive and interesting words can you think of for the action of walking? Spend 3 minutes writing a list of these words in your jotter. Then compare your list with the words other people in your class thought of.

Word choice and connotation

A writer who has a rich, varied and wide vocabulary is able to make clever decisions about the skill we call **word choice**. Of course, all the words that a writer uses are chosen in some way, but when we talk about **word choice** as a technique we mean that certain words are very carefully and deliberately chosen to obtain particular effects, or to suggest particular meanings.

When we answer questions about a writer's word choice, we are using our knowledge of the **connotations** of words. The **connotations** of a word are the ideas that a word suggests to us.

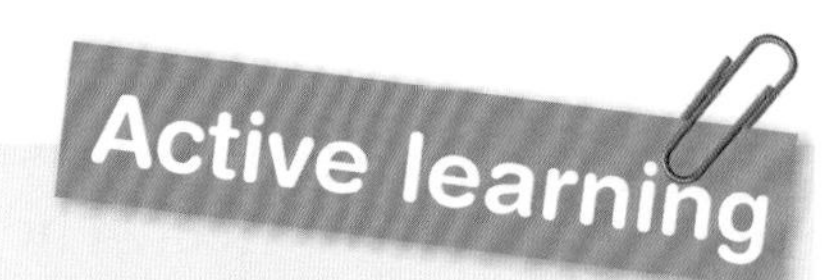

Answer the following questions to show that you understand the **connotations** of certain words:

In the poems about hungry monsters we worked with verbs about eating.

1 What does the word 'gobbled' suggest about the way someone eats?

2 What does the word 'nibbled' suggest about the way someone eats?

We also thought about words for the action of walking.

3 What does the word 'stroll' suggest about the way someone walks?

4 What does the word 'hike' suggest about the way someone walks?

5 What does the word 'storm' suggest about the way someone walks?

Now answer these questions about words and their connotations:

6 What does the word 'scribble' suggest about the way someone draws a picture?

7 What does the word 'scrawl' suggest about the way someone writes?

8 What does the word 'fold' suggest about the way someone stirs a bowl of cake mix?

9 What does the word 'beat' suggest about the way someone stirs a bowl of cake mix?

10 What does the word 'slumber' suggest about the way someone sleeps?

11 What does the word 'nap' suggest about the way someone sleeps?

12 What does the word 'aroma' suggest about a smell?

13 What does the word 'stink' suggest about a smell?

14 What is the difference in meaning between the words 'overweight' and 'obese'?

15 What is the difference in meaning between the words 'pretty' and 'gorgeous'?

16 What is the difference in meaning between the words 'large' and 'enormous'?

First, read the following passage right through once. Then answer the questions that follow. There are lots of them! Most of them are about the writer's vocabulary and word choice, but you will also get an opportunity to show that you remember what you learned already about purpose. The paragraphs have been numbered to help you.

My dog stole my tractor

1 I've been farming sheep and cattle on this hillside in South Lanarkshire, Scotland, for 54 years. I use a John Deere Gator to get about – a utility vehicle bigger than a quad bike but smaller than a tractor. It's just a little truck with a roll cage, really – it does about 40 mph. My black and white border collie, Don, always sits beside me in the passenger seat. I've had him about 5 years now, since he was a pup. He's not the best dog I've had, but he's good enough.

2 It was a little after 8 a.m. when I spotted the lost lamb. I was in the top field, near where the motorway cuts through my land. The lamb had become separated from its mother. You have to keep them paired up, so I hopped out of the Gator to tend to it while Don stayed in his seat and watched me through the back window. That's the way we always work – I leave the door open and if I need any help from Don, I shout and out he comes.

Farmer Tom Hamilton, with his dog Don and the Gator utility vehicle that Don 'stole'

3 Lamb and mother reunited, I turned back to the Gator only to see it lurch suddenly away from me. This was so unexpected it took me a moment to process what was happening. I'd put the handbrake on when I jumped out, as I always do, and I knew Don wasn't able to release it – had it not engaged properly? I still don't know how, but it was clear that Don had somehow set the vehicle in motion. He was watching me, without any obvious concern, as the Gator careered away.

4 My stomach lurched as I saw where it was heading. I didn't even have time to call out, and anyway, what could I have said? My heart seemed to freeze in my chest as I gave chase, praying I'd be able to throw myself through the open door before disaster struck.

➜

5 There were no more than 150 yards to the motorway, and the gap was closing fast. I'm pretty fit for a 77-year-old, but even before I tripped I knew I stood no chance of catching up. I fell heavily, winding myself, and was still picking myself up as the Gator crashed through a wooden fence and plunged out of view. The last thing I saw before it disappeared was Don's face, gazing benignly back at me.

6 Beyond the fence was a steep, 30 ft bank, and at the bottom of that the northbound carriageway of the M74, teeming with rush-hour commuters. I could hear the roar of the traffic. I listened for the sound of an impact or of screeching brakes as I dashed towards the fence, but none came.

7 Heart in mouth, I reached the fence and peered over. Below me, a man in a high-visibility jacket was standing in the road, holding his arms wide to stop oncoming vehicles. He had broken off from a group of road maintenance workers on the hard shoulder.

The Gator was resting against the crash barrier in the central reservation, having miraculously crossed three busy lanes. I couldn't see Don, but as I approached the Gator he leapt out on to the road, apparently unhurt, and dashed back up the bank and out of sight.

8 The Gator's engine was still running as I hauled myself into the driver's seat. The windscreen had been smashed. I was dimly aware of the growing tailback of cars and lorries as I backed it round and drove it towards the bank. One of the workmen came running to stop me, but I paid him no attention – I suppose I must have been in shock. I'd expected to see a pile-up, and feared there would be casualties. That outcome was still playing out in my head, even as I drove back through the hole in the fence.

9 By the time the police arrived, the motorway was running normally again. I couldn't quite believe my luck – it turned out I'd broken a rib when I fell and Don had a slight limp for a couple of days, but the outcome could have been awful. Don was given a special meal that night – I didn't want him thinking I was angry with him.

10 As soon as the Gator's windscreen was fixed, I started using it again, and he jumped in with me as happily as he always has. I'm extra vigilant now; no matter how calm my dog proved in that near-disastrous situation, I don't think my heart could take another.

Now answer the questions:

Read paragraph 1 again.

1 a) Which word in the second sentence tells us the Gator is basic and useful?

b) Look at the third sentence. Which two separate words show that the Gator is not a very special vehicle?

Now read paragraph 2 again.

2 a) Which word tells us the writer was not actually looking for a lost lamb?

b) Which word tells us his farm is divided by the road?

c) What does the word 'hopped' suggest about the way he got out of the Gator?

d) Which word tells us the writer knew that the lamb needed care?

Now read paragraph 3 again.

3 a) What does the word 'lurch' suggest about the way the Gator moved away?

b) '… it was clear that Don had somehow set the vehicle in motion.' Which single word here backs up the idea that the writer does not know how Don did this?

c) The writer says the Gator 'careered' away. What does this word suggest about the way the vehicle moved?

Now read paragraph 4 again.

4 a) Which two separate phrases in this paragraph tell us that the writer felt shocked?

b) What does the word 'throw' tell us about how he would have to move to get back into the vehicle?

Now read paragraph 5 again.

5 a) What does the word 'winding' tell us about how the writer felt when he fell?

b) What does the word 'plunged' tell us about the way the Gator went out of sight?

Now read paragraph 6 again.

6 a) What does the word 'teeming' suggest about the motorway?

b) What does the word 'roar' suggest about the traffic?

c) What does the word 'dashed' suggest about how the writer moved?

Now read paragraph 7 again.

7 a) What does the word 'miraculously' suggest about the way the Gator crossed the motorway?

b) Which word in this paragraph tells us that Don the dog seemed to be all right?

→

Now read paragraph 8 again.

8 a) Which word in the third sentence tells us the writer was not really paying attention?

b) Which word in this paragraph means the same as 'queue'?

Now read paragraph 9 again.

9 Which word in the second sentence tells us Don was not badly hurt?

Now read paragraph 10 again.

10 Which expression in this paragraph tells us the writer is always very careful now?

Formal and informal

So far in our studies of wonderful words we have learned about what a vivid and varied **vocabulary** we have in the English language, and also about how writers use careful **word choice** and the **connotations**, the suggestions, of certain words to put their ideas across to the reader.

Now we are going to learn about an idea sometimes called **register**. This does not mean the list of names that your teacher checks at the start of the lesson to see if everyone is here. When we talk about **register** in English, we mean that writers have chosen to use a particular set or group of language, and particularly that they have made a choice between writing **formally** or **informally**.

Let's start with some definitions so you'll get what I mean here.

Formal English tends to be more correct and exact. It may use longer or more complex sentences. When we speak or write **formally** we may use more complex words and structures. Formal English feels more serious. It is also usually what we call 'standard' English, the kind of English that can be used and understood by anyone who learns English anywhere in the world, rather than using regional dialect or slang. Formal English is not personal, and does not try to seem friendly.

Informal English is more chatty, natural and friendly. It's the kind of language we use when we are talking to our friends. Informal English is much more relaxed and personal. Informal English is less standard: it can use slang, and abbreviations, e.g. short versions of words, like 'you've' instead of 'you have'. It shows more of the speaker's or writer's emotions, and more of his or her personality. It may include exaggeration.

Spot check

Count three paragraphs up from here and you will find a paragraph that is just one sentence long. Read it again. Is it formal or informal? How do you know?

These two different registers of English are not right and wrong. Each one can be absolutely the right one to use in the right situation. If you wanted to text your mum for a lift you might write this:

but it would seem a little odd if you wrote this:

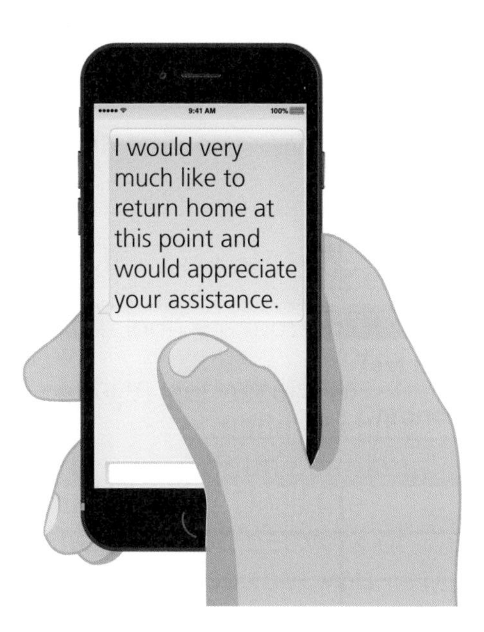

Your Physical Education teacher might think you are not very good at her subject, but if she wrote this on your report:

REPORT

Physical Education

She's hopeless at this. All right she tries, but she's still rubbish.

you might feel she wasn't taking her job, or you, seriously enough. It would be much better for her to write this:

> **REPORT**
>
> **Physical Education**
>
> She finds the subject very challenging, and, although she has made a considerable effort, I am afraid that this has not yet let to any improvement.

In that situation, formal English is the best choice.

First take a new page in your jotter and draw a line down the middle. Put the heading **FORMAL** at the top of the left-hand column, and the heading **INFORMAL** at the top of the right-hand one.

Now look at this list of situations. Decide if you would use formal or informal language in each case. Once you have decided, add the situation to the correct list in your jotter.

- Giving a close friend some advice about boyfriend problems
- Writing a letter to go with a job application
- Tagging a photo on someone's Facebook page
- Sending your dad a postcard from a school trip
- Explaining to the Head Teacher how you managed to break the staffroom window during lunchtime
- Opening your school's Christmas concert with a speech to welcome families, friends and invited guests
- Telling someone in your class on Monday morning what you did at the weekend
- Emailing a company's customer helpline to complain that a game you spent a lot of money on was damaged and would not play
- Writing an English essay about a text you have been studying in class
- Talking to a young pupil from your local primary school who seems a bit lost and upset

Next look at this list of words and phrases. Again, decide if each one is formal or informal and add it to the right list in your jotter.

- thank you
- a little girl
- Hi Mum
- you're
- I'm off
- that is unacceptable
- she's like, really?
- untrustworthy
- you are
- drunk
- thanks
- dodgy
- that's no use
- blootered
- a wee lassie
- Dear Sir or Madam
- I am leaving now
- she questioned this

Check your answers with the rest of your class so everyone has two agreed and correct lists of formal and informal language and situations.

Read this letter that a rather angry resident wanted to send to the council.

> Dear whoever,
>
> I'm totally raging about the state of our road. There's been two potholes in it since ages. I went through one of them in my car last week, and now my front wheel's trashed, my bumper's bashed, and there's a crack a mile wide in the back windscreen.
>
> You'd better send your workies soon, or I'll get my lawyer on you, and you'll get sued.
>
> Jimmy Anderson

Clearly, this is a rather informal letter. The writer will probably get much more attention, and a better response, from the council if he re-writes it more formally.

Re-write the letter using more formal English. You will need to change some of the writer's words and phrases. You may also need to add some things that he has missed out.

Compare your version with someone else's, and make improvements, before you hand it in to your teacher for marking.

Jargon and specialty

Jargon is the language that goes with particular subjects. Some jobs have a lot of jargon or specialised language that goes with them.

For example, doctors, nurses and other medical staff may use words like 'stent' or 'venflon'. They might hang a sign at the end of your hospital bed saying you are 'nil by mouth'. They might send for a 'crash team' or send a patient to the 'ICU'. They might take care of a baby in a place whose name sounds like 'skiboo' but is written down as 'SCBU'. Using jargon like this helps medical staff communicate quickly with each other. Some people think it also stops patients from feeling worried, because they may not know when the staff are concerned about them. (Other people think it can actually be very worrying to hear people using words you do not understand to talk about you when you are ill.)

Some sports, hobbies and pastimes have a lot of jargon or specialised language that goes with them. Snowboarders sometimes feel 'stoked', perhaps because they have just 'shredded' some 'gnar'. A snowboarder would rather feel 'crunchy' than 'squirrelly', and would hate to end up in a 'garage sale'.

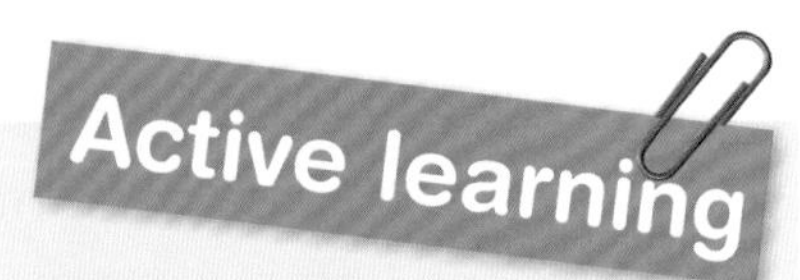

Divide your class in half, and make sure you have your teacher's permission for everyone to take their phones out.

One half of the class is going to find out the meanings of the six bits of medical jargon:

stent venflon nil by mouth crash team ICU SCBU

The other half of the class is going to find out the meanings of the six bits of snowboarding jargon:

stoked shred gnar crunchy squirrelly garage sale

Each person should stand up when he or she is finished. Which side of your class will win?

Active learning

You are going to see some speech bubbles full of jargon. Read each list and decide which job, hobby or area of life the jargon in the bubble belongs to.

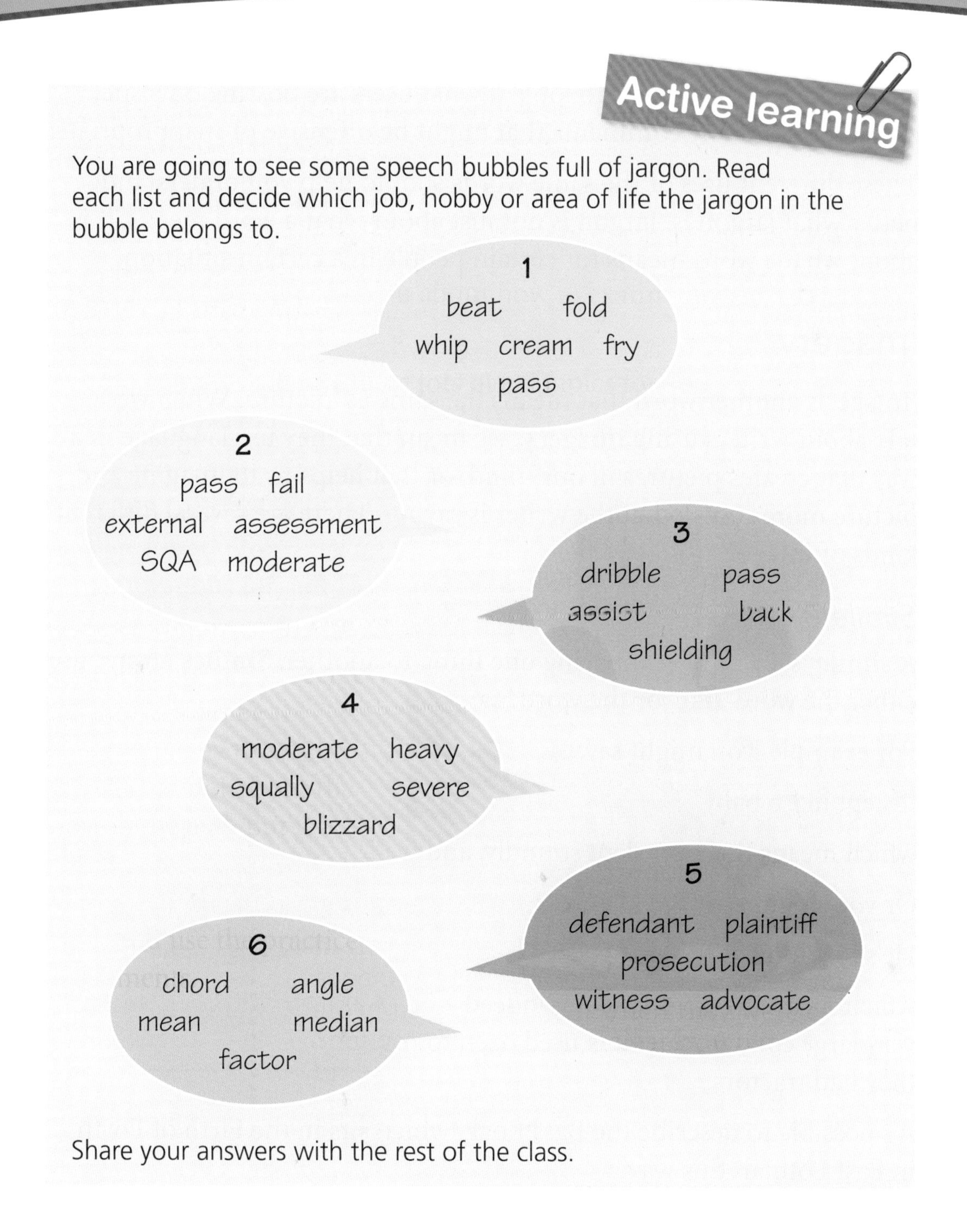

Share your answers with the rest of the class.

Did you notice that some of the words came up in more than one bubble?

When a chef talks about 'passing' something, he or she means to push food through a sieve so that any lumps are taken out. A teacher uses the word 'pass' to mean getting enough marks to achieve success in a test or an exam. In football to 'pass' means to kick the ball from one player to another on the same team.

When a teacher talks about 'moderating', he or she means he or she has marked the same piece of work as another teacher, so that they can check they are both marking their pupils fairly and to the right standard. If a weather forecaster says the wind will be 'moderate', we know it will be not too strong. In the world of social media and online chat, to 'moderate' means to look at what users are posting on a site, and to take out any comments that might be offensive or inappropriate.

These different uses of the same words should help you understand better what jargon is. Jargon is not just about what a word means, it is about what a word means for certain people in a certain situation.

Imagery

'Image' is another word that means the same as 'picture'. When we talk about writers using **imagery**, we mean that they use language in a way that creates pictures in our mind, or that helps us to imagine and picture more easily what the writer is saying. There are several different kinds of **imagery**.

Simile

A **simile** is a way of comparing one thing to another. **Similes** always use either the word '**like**' or the word '**as**'.

For example, you might say:

'I slept like a baby.'

which means that you slept soundly, and well.

Or you might write:

He's as strong as an ox.

which means he is very strong indeed – an ox is an animal a bit like a very large cow, and farmers used oxen to pull heavy machinery before they had tractors.

It's possible to describe the Bass Rock, which sits in the Firth of Forth in East Lothian this way:

It sits on the sea like a lop-sided scone.'

which makes perfect sense when you see a picture of it.

Here is a simile used to make a joke. Can you explain it?

Customer: This coffee tastes like mud.

Barista: It should; it was ground just this morning!

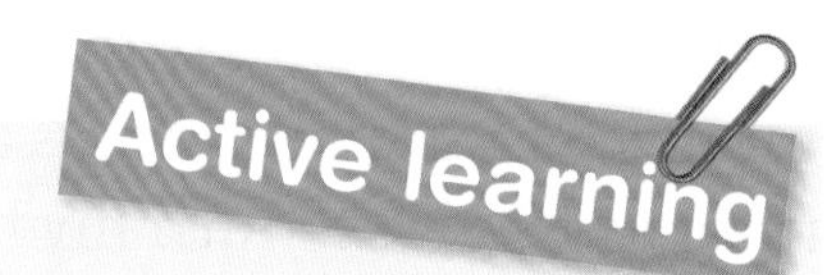

Match the object to the simile.

Objects	Similes
branches	like slow trains moving through the grass
ice	like arms waving in the sky
worms	like sheets of glass
ears	like saucers

Match the animal to the quality.

as	cheeky	as a	giraffe
	brave		bat
	tall		monkey
	blind		lion

Use the structure to describe yourself in six similes:

- I am as wild as a ______________________________
- I run like ______________________________
- I swim like ______________________________
- I talk like ______________________________
- I am as good as ______________________________
- I am as angry as ______________________________

Metaphor

Metaphors are another kind of comparison, but they are a bit stronger than similes. A simile says that one thing is like another; a **metaphor** makes a very strong comparison by saying one thing **is** another.

For example, something that is very annoying might be:

a pain in the neck

or if your classroom was very cold you might call it:

a freezer

When we use metaphors, we are usually just comparing one aspect of the thing. If I say my classroom is a freezer, I only mean that it is cold, not that it is full of chunks of frozen meat, a bag of oven chips and some ice cream. If I say that something is a pain in the neck, I only mean that it is annoying, as a sore neck would be, not that it stops me from being able to turn my head.

Explain what the following metaphors mean:

1 That girl is a monster.
2 That boy's an angel.
3 It's raining men.
4 I've got a mountain of work to do.
5 She's been battling with illness.
6 His heart is broken.
7 She's been my rock.
8 He's the light of my life.
9 She was going to do it, but she got cold feet.
10 Things were difficult to start with, but it's all plain sailing now.

First read this poem about the sea.

The Sea

The sea is a hungry dog,
Giant and grey.
He rolls on the beach all day.
With his clashing teeth and shaggy jaws
Hour upon hour he gnaws
The rumbling, tumbling stones,
And 'Bones, bones, bones, bones!'
The giant sea-dog moans,
Licking his greasy paws.

And when the night wind roars
And the moon rocks in the stormy cloud,
He bounds to his feet and snuffs and sniffs,
Shaking his wet sides over the cliffs,
And howls and hollos long and loud.

But on quiet days in May or June,
When even the grasses on the dune
Play no more their reedy tune,
With his head between his paws
He lies on the sandy shores,
So quiet, so quiet, he scarcely snores.

James Reeves

Now look carefully just at **verse 1**, and answer these questions:

1 What is the main metaphor that the writer uses in this poem?

2 Give two ways, according to the poem, that the sea is like this other thing.

3 The writer describes the sea gnawing the land 'with his clashing teeth and shaggy jaws'. What is really happening?

We will return to that poem again soon.

Personification

When we use **personification**, we talk about non-living things as if they were alive, as if they were people (or perhaps animals).

For example you could describe a Formula 1 race by saying:

The cars screamed round the circuit.

Cars cannot really scream. They do not have throats, and they do not feel scared or angry. But, by personifying the cars with the word 'screamed', we know what kind of noise came from their engines.

You could describe a storm by saying:

The wind howled.

Wind cannot really howl. It does not have a throat, and it is not a wolf. But, by personifying the wind with the word 'howled', we know what kind of noise it made.

You could describe a tree by saying:

The branches waved in the wind.

Branches cannot really wave. They do not have hands to wave with. But, by personifying the branches with the word 'waved', we can picture how they moved.

Look back again at the poem about the sea. The main metaphor of that poem – that the sea is a hungry dog – is actually a form of personification. All the way through the poem, the sea, which is not alive, is given the qualities and details of a big, shaggy dog.

Explain these examples of **personification**. To do this, you need to be able to say what is the non-living thing in each comparison, and also what living thing this is being compared to.

1. The tidal wave swallowed everything in its path.
2. When the band failed the audition their dreams died.
3. The door screeched open.
4. She hadn't eaten since breakfast and her stomach was grumbling.
5. He saw the secret signal light winking in the window.
6. The cars crawled through the roadworks.
7. The top toys have been flying off the shelves this Christmas.
8. We're not ready to play that team – they'll chew us up and spit us out.

Symbols

So far we have looked at three kinds of image: similes, metaphors and personification. All these images are based on something **imaginary**:

- If I use the **simile** of saying that someone 'swims like a fish', there is a good swimmer there, but there aren't actually any fish.
- If I use the **metaphor** of calling someone a 'monster', I mean there is a very bad person there, but there is not a big, hairy, vicious creature running around.

- If I **personify** the wind by saying it 'howled', I mean it makes a big horrible noise, but there are not actually any wolves or dogs there.

Symbols are a bit different, because they are always based on something that is **real in the world of the text**. This real thing, as well as being a detail in the story, or the poem, or the novel, also stands for another important idea.

Think about Harry Potter. At the start of the first book, his Dursley relatives make him sleep in the cupboard under the stairs. That cupboard is real in the world of the story – it is really where Harry sleeps, and it is really under the stairs of the Dursley family's house. But it is also a **symbol**. It is small, and cold, and dark, and not a suitable bedroom for an 11-year-old boy. That nasty cupboard under the stairs is a symbol for how his relatives feel about Harry. It **symbolises** the fact that they do not love or care for him.

Or think about *The Hobbit* and *The Lord of the Rings*. In the world of these books and films, the ring is real. Bilbo takes it from Smaug the dragon, and Frodo eventually has to destroy it. But the ring is also a symbol. It stands for all sorts of negative human qualities like greed and evil.

1 Look at these two pictures. They both show Christmas trees. But they **symbolise** two different sorts of Christmas. What does each tree tell us about the two different Christmases these families are going to have?

2 Look at this bunch of flowers. If a man gave these to his girlfriend, what would they say about the way he feels about her?

3 What do these things usually symbolise?

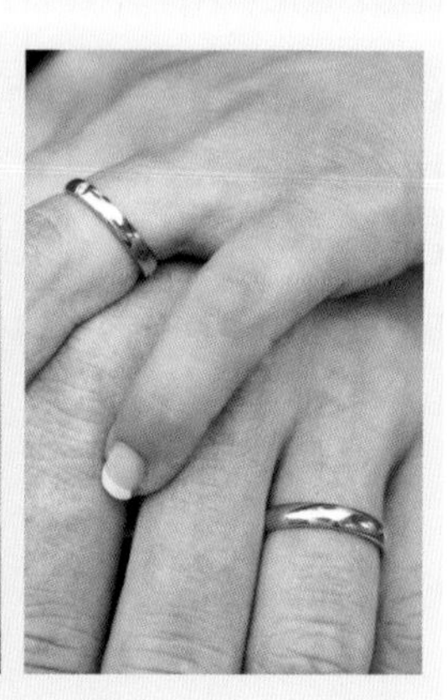

Bringing it all together

In this section you have learned about four kinds of imagery: **similes**, **metaphors**, **personification** and **symbolism**. It is time to review how well you understand these.

Read this passage from a novel, describing an unpleasant journey by sea.

The Lie Tree

The boat moved with a nauseous, relentless rhythm, like someone chewing on a rotten tooth. The islands just visible through the mist also looked like teeth, Faith decided. Not fine, clean Dover teeth, but jaded, broken teeth, jutting crookedly amid the wash of the choppy grey sea. The mailboat chugged its dogged way through the waves, greasing the sky with smoke.

The mist flattened everything and sucked out all colour. Trees became intricate smoke-hued doilies. Buildings were featureless outlines, eiderdown grey. The night before, the cliffs had been inky and massive. This morning they were grey paper. She could have thrown a stone and torn them.

The wind flattened glossy spirals in the grass, and the trees flung up their boughs like drowning sailors.

Now show your understanding of imagery by copying and completing this table in your jotter. The answers go in order through the passage. This is quite a tricky task that will really test your understanding – some of the rows have clues to help you.

Para	Quotation	Clue	Type of image
1	'The boat moved with a nauseous, relentless rhythm'	Focus on the description of the word 'rhythm'	
1	'like someone chewing on a rotten tooth'	–	
1	'jaded, broken teeth'	'Jaded' means fed up and exhausted	
1	'The mailboat chugged its dogged way'	'Dogged' means determined	
2	'The mist flattened everything and sucked out all colour'	–	
2	'Trees became intricate, smoke-hued doilies'	–	
2	'they were grey paper'	–	
3		Look at the trees	personification
3	'like drowning sailors'	–	

Now answer these questions:

1 What feeling does the writer suggest by saying that the boat's rhythm is 'nauseous'?

2 What is the writer trying to make us feel when she says the boat's movement is, 'like someone chewing on a rotten tooth'?

3 What is the writer suggesting about the boat by writing that it moved in a 'dogged' way?

4 What is the writer suggesting about the trees when she says 'they were grey paper'?

5 What is the writer suggesting about the trees when she says they 'flung up their boughs like drowning sailors'?

Sound effects

When you were learning to read, you probably read the words out loud to yourself. Even now that you are older, and you read most things to yourself, you do sort of still hear writers' words inside your head. Writers know that we read this way so, even when they are creating words that we will only read on a page, they often use **sound effects**. We are going to learn about some of these **sound effect** techniques now.

Alliteration

Alliteration is when writers use two or more words, close to each other, which begin with the same sound. For example:

wild, windy weather　　or　　cosy cottage

Writers love alliteration because it is very catchy. This sound effect makes writers' words and ideas stick to our brains more quickly and easily. Because it is so memorable, alliteration is often used in headlines. Imagine an Edinburgh derby football game. If the team from Easter Road won, the headline might be:

HAPPY HIBBEES HAMMER HOPELESS HEARTS

but if the game went the other way, and the winners were playing at home, the headline could be:

TYNECASTLE TEAM TRIUMPHS

Alliteration is also popular in adverts. One for frozen peas described them as being:

sweet as the moment when the pod went pop

Can you think of any more alliterative adverts? Put your hand up and be ready to tell your class about them.

Some company names or brand names use alliteration. For example:

Krispy Kreme　　or　　PowerPoint

Can you think of any more alliterative company names or brand names? Put your hand up and be ready to tell the class about them.

Some tongue twisters use alliteration. For example:

Round and round the rugged rock the ragged rascal ran

or

She sells sea shells by the sea shore

> Can you think of any more alliterative tongue twisters? Put your hand up and be ready to tell the class about them.

Some names of films or TV programmes use alliteration. For example:

Batman Begins   or   Breaking Bad   or   Guardians of the Galaxy

> Can you think of any more alliterative film or programme titles? Put your hand up and be ready to tell the class about them.

Some titles of songs use alliteration. For example:

Heartbreak Hotel (Elvis Presley) or Hungry Heart (Bruce Springsteen)

> Can you think of any more alliterative song titles? Put your hand up and be ready to tell the class about them.

Overnight activity

You have until your next English lesson to do this. Bring in a piece of music to play to your teacher. The song must have alliteration in its title. If you are very lucky, and your teacher is very kind, you might even get a prize or reward for doing this.

Now that you understand what **alliteration** is, you are going to create some of your own.

My name is Jane, and I am a fairly cheerful sort of person. I am also fond of fruit and a sucker for sweet stuff (there's some more alliteration!) so I could describe a shopping trip like this:

I'm joyful Jane and when I went shopping I bought some juicy jam.

Your teacher will give you 2 minutes to work out an alliteration that describes you, and another alliteration for something you could buy.

At the end of the 2 minutes, everyone in your class should read out their alliterative sentence.

The key reason why writers use alliteration is because it is so catchy. It grabs our attention and makes us focus on the writer's ideas.

Now it is time to meet our next sound effect technique.

Onomatopoeia

Onomatopoeia is the language technique used when the sound of a word matches its meaning. Lots of words for the noises animals make are examples of **onomatopoeia**. For example:

woof or hiss or miaow

> Can you think of any more onomatopoeic animal sounds? Put your hand up and be ready to tell the class about them.

Lots of words for noises are examples of **onomatopoeia**. For example:

bang or clank or thump

> Can you think of any more onomatopoeic words for noises? Put your hand up and be ready to tell the class about them.

Lots of words for actions or movements are examples of onomatopoeia. For example:

swish or whirl or tap

> Can you think of any more onomatopoeic words for actions or movements? Put your hand up and be ready to tell the class about them.

My favourite example of onomatopoeia is 'splash'. You can really hear the sound of the pebble hitting the surface of the pond in the opening sp-sound, and the soft ripples of the water circling outwards in the -sh at the end of the word.

Overnight activity

Onomatopoeia is a hard word to spell, which means that people will be very impressed if you can spell it. Write the word down now in your homework diary, or, if you have your teacher's permission, you might enter it into your phone.

You have until your next English lesson to memorise the spelling. As you come into the lesson, go up to your teacher (as long as he or she is not too busy!) and spell the word quietly. If you are very lucky, and your teacher is very kind, you might even get a prize or reward for doing this.

The key reason why writers use onomatopoeia is because it is so vivid and lively. It grabs our attention and makes us almost feel and hear the words as well as reading them with our eyes.

Now it is time to meet our next sound effect technique.

Rhyme

You will know about this technique already. So, instead of giving a definition, here is a question.

Imagine a Martian arrived in your classroom and told you he had been sent to Earth to learn about our weird and wonderful (more alliteration!) human languages. How would you explain to him what rhyme is?

- **First** work on your own. Write down a definition of what **rhyme** is.
- **Now** work with a partner. Compare your definitions and come up with a shared, even better explanation.
- **Next**, check if you have included any examples. Make sure you have at least two different examples of rhyme along with your definition.
- **Finally**, share your definitions and examples with the rest of your class. Your teacher might decide that the class does not need to hear every pair's definition, because it should be possible for the class to agree quite quickly what rhyme is. But every pair should get a chance to give at least one of their examples.

Like alliteration, rhyme is very catchy and memorable, so it is also often used in advertising. One famous chocolate bar used to have the slogan:

A Mars a day helps you work, rest and play

and a chain of travel agents used the slogan:

Don't just book it, Thomas Cook it

Can you think of any more rhyming advertising slogans? Put your hand up and be ready to tell the class about them.

Now that we are sure we all know what rhyme is, you are going to learn a way of marking it on a text. We do this using letters, and we take a new letter for each new rhyming sound.

Look at this famous nursery rhyme:

Mary had a little lamb
Its fleece was white as snow
And everywhere that Mary went
The lamb was sure to go.

The first line ends with 'lamb'. We will call that sound **A**. The second line ends with 'snow'. That does not rhyme with 'lamb' so it is a new sound. We will call that sound **B**. The third line ends with 'went'. That is another new sound that does not rhyme with either of the previous sounds, so we will call it **C**. The last line ends with 'go'. That rhymes with 'snow' which was our **A** sound, so we will use that **A** again. The poem can be marked up looking like this:

Mary had a little lamb	**A**
Its fleece was white as snow	**B**
And everywhere that Mary went	**C**
The lamb was sure to go.	**A**

Here is a slightly naughty version of the same poem. Starting again from **A**, mark up the rhyme scheme.

Mary had a little lamb
A lobster and some prunes
A piece of pie, a glass of milk
And then some macaroons.
It made the naughty waiters grin
To see her order so
And when they carried Mary out
Her face was white as snow.

Share your answers with the rest of the class and make sure everyone agrees.

Bonus question: Can you explain the difference in meaning between the word 'had' the way it is used in line 1 of the classic version of the poem, and the way it is used in the naughty version?

Bringing it all together

In this section you have learned about three kinds of sound effect technique: **alliteration**, **onomatopoeia** and **rhyme**. It is time to review how well you understand these.

You are going to read the beginning of a poem by Edgar Allan Poe. Your teacher might be able to give you a copy of it on paper, so that you can make notes or marks on the text.

Task 1

First of all, read the poem, 'The Bells'. It has a really wonderful rhythm, so you should make sure you hear it read out loud. Perhaps your teacher could read it first, and then other people in the class could have a go at reading it.

Task 2

Divide your class in half. One half of the class should look at verse 1 of the poem, while the other half looks at verse 2.

Make sure you know which half of the poem you are looking at. Using the letters A, B, C and so on, mark up the rhyme scheme for your verse, the way that you learned to do when you looked at 'Mary Had a Little Lamb'.

Now look at your rhyming sounds. Which sound does Poe use most often in your verse?

Share your answers in the class.

Task 3

Now swap verses. The people who looked at verse 1 before should now examine verse 2, and so on.

In your verse look for, and make a list of:

- any examples of alliteration
- any examples of onomatopoeia.

Share your answers with the rest of the class.

The Bells

I

Hear the sledges with the bells –
Silver bells!
What a world of merriment their melody foretells!
How they tinkle, tinkle, tinkle,
In the icy air of night!
While the stars that oversprinkle
All the heavens, seem to twinkle
With a crystalline delight;
Keeping time, time, time,
In a sort of Runic rhyme,
To the tintinnabulation that so musically wells
From the bells, bells, bells, bells,
Bells, bells, bells –
From the jingling and the tinkling of the bells

II

Hear the mellow wedding bells
Golden bells!
What a world of happiness their harmony foretells!
Through the balmy air of night
How they ring out their delight!
From the molten-golden notes,
And all in tune,
What a liquid ditty floats
To the turtle-dove that listens, while she gloats
On the moon!
Oh, from out the sounding cells,
What a gush of euphony voluminously wells!
How it swells!
How it dwells
On the Future! how it tells
Of the rapture that impels
To the swinging and the ringing
Of the bells, bells, bells,
Of the bells, bells, bells, bells,
Bells, bells, bells –
To the rhyming and the chiming of the bells!

Overnight activity

We have only used this poem to help us look at sound effects, but it has a wonderful **vocabulary** as well. There are some words in it that you probably do not know:

tintinnabulation   balmy   ditty   euphony

Write these words down now in your homework diary, or, if you have your teacher's permission, you might enter them into your phone.

You have until your next English lesson to do this. Find out the meaning of at least one of these words, and be able to explain it to your class without having to look at any notes. If you are very lucky, and your teacher is very kind, you might even get a prize or reward for doing this.

Sentence types

We are going to learn soon about different sorts of sentences. However, let us just check first of all that we are sure we know what a sentence is. Here are two easy questions:

1 How do we recognise the start of a sentence?

2 How do we recognise the end of a sentence?

But it is what we find in between the start and the end that really makes a sentence. One way of explaining it is to say that **a sentence is a group of words that make sense together, and one of the words should be a verb, a doing word**.

So, this is a sentence:

Ben was sitting on the edge of the harbour, with his feet over the water.

The line below, however, is not a sentence, even though the person who wrote it used a capital letter and a full stop:

Sitting on the edge of the harbour.

because those words do not make sense on their own together. They only make sense with other sentences around them; for example, like the question, 'Where was Ben when you saw him on Saturday?'

Now that we have checked that we know what a sentence is, we are going to learn about different kinds of sentences.

Statement

A **statement** is a sentence that gives a fact or a piece of information, or that gives an opinion in a clear way. The sentence that we saw before:

Ben was sitting on the edge of the harbour, with his feet over the water.

is a **statement**. It tells us where Ben was, and what he was doing.

Here are some more statements. Read them over and decide which ones are **statements of fact**, and which ones are **statements of opinion**:

1. Teenagers are not good at getting out of bed in the morning.
2. Rats are horrible, disgusting, evil little rodents.
3. When it was released in 2015, *Star Wars: The Force Awakens* quickly became the most successful film ever made.
4. Designer clothes and accessories are expensive.
5. Scotland is a small country, with a population of about 5.5 million people.
6. *The Force Awakens* is the best film in the *Star Wars* series because it has got the best female character.
7. Designer clothes and accessories are over-priced.
8. It is important for teenagers to get enough sleep as their brains and bodies are going through many rapid changes.
9. Rats are rodents.
10. Scotland is the best little country in the world.

Statements are the most common kind of sentence in English. Most of the sentences in this book so far are statements. All three sentences in this paragraph are statements.

Question

You can recognise **questions** in someone else's writing because they end with a question mark. You should use a question mark instead of a full stop when you put **questions** in your own writing.

You are going to play the question game. Sit with a partner.

Person number 1 asks number 2 a question. Number 2 has to answer with a question, so the game could go like this:

1 How are you today?

2 Why do you want to know?

1 Don't you want to tell me?

2 Why are you so interested?

Play the game. How long can you keep it going?

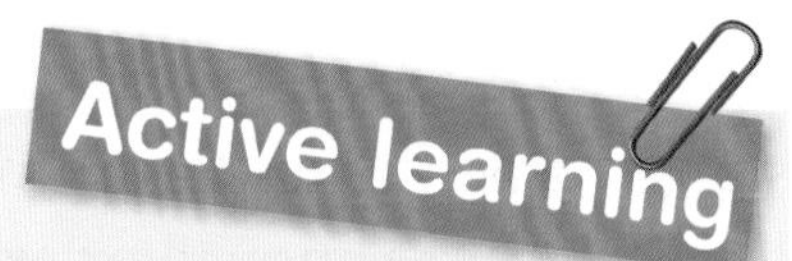

Read this short passage. Some of the sentences in it are questions, but the writer has forgotten to put in any of the question marks.

- Where should the writer use question marks?
- How many question marks do you need to add altogether?

When I saw Ben on Saturday, he was sitting on the edge of the harbour with his feet over the water. I asked him what he was doing later.

'I don't know,' he said. 'What do you want to do.'

'Do you feel like going sailing.'

'Maybe,' he said, 'but aren't you worried about the weather forecast.'

I hadn't heard it, so I asked him what was making him nervous.

'Don't you know. They say there's going to be a storm this afternoon. Do you really want to be out at sea if that happens.'

There are lots of questions in this book, and you are supposed to answer them as you work through the pages to show that you understand what you are learning. However, writers and speakers often use something called a **rhetorical question**, which is a question that does not expect an answer. **Rhetorical questions** are there to make the reader, or the listener, think. Writers and speakers use **rhetorical questions** to get us to connect more with what they are writing or saying. Sometimes the writer or speaker might go on to answer his or her own rhetorical question.

For example, a politician might start a speech like this:

Sometimes writers use a number of questions together. This can suggest that the writer is unsure about a lot of things, or that there is lots we do not know. For example:

Archaeologists are still puzzled about Stonehenge. How was it built? Why are the stones arranged as they are? What were these ancient people thinking as they gathered there in this special place?

Instruction

Some sentences tell us what to do. They give **instructions.**

You are going to play a game. One person from your class needs to volunteer to follow instructions from other pupils.

Get your volunteer to come and stand at the front of the class. They should pick one person in the class, and let that person give them an instruction to follow, for example: 'Open the door, go out into the corridor, and then come back in again.'

The first instructor can choose who gives the second instruction. The second instructor can choose who gives the third instruction, and so on. When your teacher thinks you have played for long enough, decide who gave the most interesting instruction.

WARNING! If your teacher thinks you have given a silly or unsuitable instruction, he or she will not make the volunteer do what you say, but will make you come and stand at the front of the class and follow the rest of the instructions instead.

Certain kinds of writing use a lot of instructions – for example recipes. Certain kinds of speech use a lot of instructions – for example, a coach standing at the side of the pitch during a sports match would shout instructions to the team.

Minor sentences

Think back to our definition of a sentence on page 48. We said that a sentence is 'a group of words that make sense together, and one of the words should be a verb, a doing word'.

Minor sentences, in a sense, are not really sentences at all. A **minor sentence** is a sentence that does not have good grammar, because it does not have a main verb. So, a **minor sentence** is a group of words that do not really make full sense on their own together; a sentence that we only really understand because of the other sentences round it.

Minor sentences are usually short, because it is quite hard to write much in English without using a main verb. Look at this example, where the minor sentences are in bold:

She kept going. **Scrambling. Climbing. Staggering.** She would never give up until she was safely out of the valley and back on the road to the city.

That does not mean that every short sentence is a minor sentence.

Stop!

is a very short sentence, but it is not minor, because the word 'Stop!' is a main verb that makes sense on its own.

Read the following passage. There are eight minor sentences in it. Can you find them?

An empty room. A dusty old wooden trunk in the corner by the window. This must be the place.

Carefully, she lifted the lid. The hinges creaked. She pulled out the contents, item by item, laying them on the floor. Heaps of ancient cashmere sweaters with moth holes in them. Letters written on paper as thin as onion skins. Tickets for plays starring actors she had never heard of.

She found it at the very bottom. She could have missed it completely. It looked so ordinary. Just a blue envelope, with AIR MAIL on the corner. For some reason, she slipped her fingers inside, and felt the edges of a thin pile of sheets of paper. Bank notes.

Hardly able to breathe for excitement, she counted them. She counted again. Each note was worth a hundred pounds. There were ten notes. A thousand pounds.

Minor sentences can be very effective, because they can seem quite dramatic. They grab the reader's attention. But you should not use them too often in your own writing, or your teacher might just think that you do not know how to write a proper sentence.

Bringing it all together

In this section you have learned about four kinds of sentence: **statement**, **question**, **instruction** and **minor sentence**. It is time to review how well you understand these.

You are going to read a passage. Your teacher might be able to give you a copy of it on paper, so that you can make notes or marks on the text.

As you read, mark up the passage:

- Draw a dotted line under the statements. This is a statement.
- Draw a bubble round the questions. Is this a question?
- Underline the instructions. Go on, do it!
- Draw a wiggly line under the minor sentences. Like this.

Here's the passage:

They stood at the top of the steep slope, peering at the river far below. Hannah could feel herself wobbling, as if something was pulling her downwards. Horrible. She shuddered.

'What should we do?' Jamie's words broke into her thoughts.

'I don't know.'

'We have to get away from those people.'

CLUE: sometimes you might need to use two of the markings at once, because a sentence might belong to two of the four types.

'Do you think I don't understand that?' Hannah snapped.

'Then do something!'

She looked at him, staring up at her. Her little brother. Wee Jamie, though not so wee now. It was her job to protect him. Then she turned and looked back, over her shoulder. There was something there. What? A cloud? Mist rolling in? No, it was smoke. Billowing, racing, choking smoke. And it was coming closer.

'Will you do something for me Jamie?' She took hold of his hand as she said it. He hated holding her hand; he said ten was far too old for hand-holding. She didn't just take his hand, she gripped it.

'What do you want me to do?' He hadn't seen the smoke yet.

'Run!'

Person

If you have ever written a story, you have made a decision (whether you realise it or not) about which **person** to write in.

The **first person** is when the narrator is **speaking or writing about himself or herself.**

You can recognise first person writing because the narrator will use words like '**I**', '**me**', '**my**' and '**mine**'. If the narrator is telling us about a group of people that he or she belongs to, you will see words like '**we**', '**us**', '**our**' and '**ours**'.

First person is often used by people describing personal experiences, or telling part of their life story. It feels as if the narrator is talking directly to us. Using **first person** can make the reader feel very involved.

Here is an extract from near the start of the biography of the footballer Niamh McKevitt. Her dad used to take her brother to Soccer Skills sessions and her mother was out at work, so Niamh had to come too. Her dad suggested she should join in, instead of just watching.

> I hadn't thought about actually playing before, but Evan seemed to be having fun so I decided that next week I would play too. When we turned up the following Saturday a lot of the boys – and there were only boys – were much older than me and seemed twice my size. I was genuinely scared and spent the first session hiding in the far corners of the pitch, trying to stay away from the biggest boys and – most importantly – from the ball.
>
> If it wasn't for the coaches, that first session could have been one of the longest hours of my life. I really didn't take to it at all. I had very little natural ability I could only really kick the ball when it wasn't moving, although surprisingly I wasn't the worst player there by any means.
>
> *From* Playing With the Boys *by Niamh McKevitt*

Although first person is wonderful for making readers feel involved, it does mean that the writer can only write from one point of view. The writer can only write about the things that the narrator – the storytelling character – does, or knows.

The **second person** is for speaking or writing **to** somebody.

You can recognise second person writing because the narrator will use words like '**you**', '**your**' and '**yours**'.

Second person is used for talking or writing to people. It is often used for giving instructions. For example:

> If you are going to make a cake, you should prepare properly first. You should read over the recipe, and make sure you have all the ingredients and equipment you need. Also, check how long it takes to bake, and ask yourself if you have enough time.

The **third person** is for speaking or writing **about** somebody else.

You can recognise third person writing because the narrator will use words like '**he**', '**she**', '**it**' and '**they**'. You will also notice words like '**him**', '**her**', '**them**', '**their**' and '**theirs**'.

We saw earlier that first person writing restricts the point of view. Third person gives the writer a lot more freedom. The writer can describe all sorts of different characters, places and events. For example:

> The dog padded down the alleyway, sniffing its way along the edges of the buildings. Something in there smelled interesting. The closer the dog got to the bin, the more wildly its tail wagged.
>
> At the other end of the alley, Detective Inspector Jemma Hastie stood watching the dog. She trusted it. If there was even the faintest trace of their suspect, the Alsatian would sniff it out. The thought cheered her up. It was time she got some kind of break in this case.
>
> Alan watched from the front seat of his car across the road. It was risky for him to be there when the police were so close, but he had to see what they were up to. Would they find the bag he'd stuffed in behind the dumped mattress? He hoped not. What was in that bag was valuable, and he had to get it back.
>
> Just then, a fist banged on the passenger side window.

Bringing it all together

In this section you have learned about the three **persons** we can write in: **first**, **second** and **third**. It is time to review how well you understand these.

Task 1

Read the following sentences. Decide if they are **first**, **second** or **third person**:

1. It rained hard all that day, and all next day too.
2. I've never been to New York, though I've wanted to go for years.
3. You nearly ran me right off the road.
4. She had no idea how to do her Maths homework, and the revision for her Science test made no sense at all.
5. If you keep going all the way to the end of the street, and then cross at the traffic lights, you'll find the cinema just in front of you on the left.
6. I never drink milk, I hate eggs, and I'm not that fond of cheese either.

7 The next time I go snowboarding, I'm going to take my own board instead of hiring one when I get there.

8 You should check over what you have written before you hand it in, so that you can fix any little mistakes in spelling and punctuation.

9 He turned the phone over and over in his jacket pocket, willing it to ring.

10 The longest, hardest, most exciting day of my life actually started out quite normally.

11 Those of you on the left side of the games hall can put bibs on and be the red team.

12 They were sitting in the front row of the cinema, passing the bag of popcorn back and forward along the row, when the fire alarm suddenly went off.

Task 2

Now you are going to re-write some of those sentences:

A Re-write sentence 2 into third person, using 'he'.

B Re-write sentence 4 into first person.

C Re-write sentence 6 into third person, using 'she'.

D Re-write sentence 9 into first person.

E Re-write sentence 10 into third person, using 'she'.

Task 3

1 Using first person, write five sentences to describe your day so far.

2 Using second person, write directions to help someone get from the classroom you are in now to the main door of your school.

3 Using third person, write a description of the first human being you spoke to today.

So far in this book you have worked through two chapters that have let you concentrate on two keys ways of responding to what we read.

- In Chapter 1 you learned about writers' **ideas and details**, and how we can show that we understand these.
- In this chapter, Chapter 2, you have been learning about writers' **language and style**. We have looked at some of the techniques writers can use, and the effects they get from using them.

In the rest of this book, you will get the opportunity to use what you have learned. There will be 15 passages for you to read, with questions to answer after each passage. Some of the passages will be fiction; others will be non-fiction. Some of the tasks will be quite straightforward; others will be more challenging.

Passages and Questions

In this part of the book, you will find a number of practice tests. Doing these tests will allow you to use and show your close reading skills.

The tests are designed to look quite a lot like the more formal tests you might do a little further up the school. The first three, *Your Rights as a Shopper*, *Cream of the Crop* and *A Great Escape* are quite like the Reading tests that pupils do for National 3 English. The remaining assessments aim to give you an idea of what you might find at National 4 and beyond, with assessments 13–15 being the most challenging.

Some of the questions are laid out with spaces for you to write your answers in, because some of the real National 3 and 4 tests that you will meet higher up the school are like this. Obviously you are *never* going to write on this book, but your teacher might give you a photocopy of the question and answer pages to write on. If not, you can easily write the answers on lined paper or in your jotter.

The tests will get a bit harder as you work through this section of the book. This might mean that the later passages are longer than the earlier ones. It might mean that the questions are more difficult. Or it might mean that you are no longer given quite as much shape and structure for filling in your answers, but that you have to write the answers more independently instead.

Before you start, two pieces of advice:

1 Always read the whole passage right through before you answer any of the questions. If a question tells you to look at a certain part of the passage, go back and read that bit again before you answer the question.

2 Watch out for any words in bold in the questions. These are telling you about things you have to pay particular attention to.

Assessment 1

Your Rights as a Shopper

It's a contract

When you buy something from a shop, or pay for a service (like a train fare or haircut) you are making an agreement, known in law as a contract.

The contract means that, in return for the money that you pay, the goods you buy should do everything you can reasonably expect and, in particular, all that the seller and manufacturer claim.

What about your rights if the goods you have bought are faulty?

The Sale of Goods Act

The law applying to most everyday purchases is the Sale of Goods Act. It says that when you buy goods from a shop or trader they must …

… be of saleable quality

This means that they must be free of faults and not scratched or damaged, and equally applies to goods bought in a sale. However, this rule does not apply if the fault was pointed out by the sales assistant, or if you inspected the item and had a good opportunity to discover the fault. Second-hand goods bought from a shop or trader must also be of satisfactory quality.

… be fit for all their intended purposes

This means that they must do what the seller, packaging, or advertisements claim. A watch sold as waterproof should not stop if you forget to take it off in the shower.

These protections do not apply if you bought the goods privately (e.g. through a small ad). In this case, it is the buyer's responsibility to decide the quality of what she or he wants to buy.

… match the description

The goods must be the same as the description on the packaging or advertisement, or given by the assistant at the time of sale. A bracelet marked solid silver must be just that.

This rule also applies to second-hand goods, and goods sold privately.

Questions

1 a) This article uses a lot of formal language. Give one example of a formal word or expression that the writer uses.

____

b) Why is it appropriate for the writer to use formal English in this article?

____

____

____

2 Read the section under the heading '**... be of saleable quality**'. Tick the table to show if this rule applies to these situations:

Situation	Must goods be of saleable quality?
You buy something from a shop at full price	
The sales assistant tells you there is something wrong with the goods	
You buy something from a second-hand dealer	
You buy something in a shop's sale	
You inspect the item before you buy	

3 Read the section under the heading '**... be fit for all their intended purposes**'. Using **your own words** as much as possible, explain what it means if we say that something we buy is 'fit for purpose'.

____

____

____

4 The article mentions goods that are sold 'privately'. What does the word 'privately' mean in the way that the passage uses it?

____

____

5 Do you think this is a useful article? Tick one answer:

Yes ☐

No ☐

Give a reason for your answer based on the text.

____

____

____

Assessment 2

Cream of the Crop

The following article appeared in a Scottish newspaper.

Retro cans are cream of the crop

1 A sweet-toothed dad claims to have the last surviving original cans of Creamola Foam.

2 Roddy Nicoll has tucked away two ageing cans of the legendary drink for years – but now plans to sell them to the highest bidder on an online auction website.

3 He has a rare unopened tin can of the lemon drink from the 1970s. He also has a still-drinkable plastic can of the raspberry version dating from the 1990s.

4 The 49-year-old father of four from Yoker, Glasgow, said: 'The cans were the pride of my collection of Scottish confectionery memorabilia, but I have decided to let them go as my wife and I are near 50. They are two true pieces of modern Scottish history. The time has come for them to move on to either a private collection, a museum, or the hands of whoever wants to be the last Scot to ever taste the original real thing or pop the wee paper seal on the top of a can for the last time.'

The next article appeared in the same paper a few days later.

Gee-fizz! tin hits £350

5 One of the last known unopened cans of Creamola Foam has sold for as much as £350. The brightly coloured fizzy drink mixture was snapped up by a mystery buyer on eBay.

6 *Metro* told last week how Glasgow couple Roddy and Janice Nicoll were putting the lemon-flavoured mixture up for sale after storing it in a safe for the last 40 years.

7 The rare tin was made in the 1970s and was a favourite of children across Scotland. It cost just 10p at the time and promised on the can to make '10 big drinks' – although it is not known whether it is still drinkable as it went out of date decades ago.

8 The can had a starting price of £10 but a frenzy of interest saw a total of 43 bids push the price up to £345 just moments before the auction ended. Postage costs took the total to £350.95. An earlier bid offering £900 for the crystals was withdrawn.

9 Creamola Foam was manufactured and sold in Scotland until 1998 when production ceased. It was made of powder that dissolved in cold water to create a fizzy drink with a creamy foam head. The exact recipe went missing in 2004 after the rights were bought by Nestlé.

10 The Glasgow-based Beatson Cancer Charity will receive 20% of the proceeds from the sale of the last remaining cans.

Questions

Read paragraphs 1 to 3.

1 a) Which word tells us the cans of Creamola Foam are very unusual?

____

b) Which phrase suggests Roddy Nicoll has been keeping the cans hidden?

____

c) The writer says that Roddy Nicoll 'claims' to have the last surviving cans of Creamola Foam. What does the word 'claims' suggest?

____

____

2 If you were writing a factual report about Creamola Foam, give three details that you would include to help you explain this drink to someone who does not know about it.

1 ______________________________

2 ______________________________

3 ______________________________

3 **Read paragraph 8.** The writer says there was 'a frenzy of interest' from possible buyers. Give one piece of evidence to prove this.

____

____

4 Did you find this article interesting? Tick one answer:

Yes ☐

No ☐

Give a reason for your answer based on the text.

____

____

____

Assessment 3

A Great Escape

The following article appeared in a British newspaper.

1 Another chapter was written yesterday in the history of great hamster escapes, when a pet called Mike survived three types of crushing machine and a shredder at a waste recycling plant.

2 The small rodent was left with only a minor foot injury after astonished staff discovered him limping into a final sorting area after going through a process which rips cookers and washing machines into stringy bits of metal.

3 Mike's white-knuckle ride through the Recyclo works on Deeside, north Wales, adds to the remarkable survival record of *Mesocricetus auratus* over many years. Hamsters have returned from premature burial, travelled through the post in envelopes (a highly illegal practice) and contentedly shared pet cages with poisonous snakes.

4 Mike's adventures rate highly in a sub-group of binmen sagas, particularly as Recyclo does not deal in food or similar rubbish which might attract pets.

5 'We don't get very much animal activity here,' said the plant's general manager, Tony Williams, who supervises some 400 tonnes a day of 'dry' waste. 'Some is shredded and then goes through the trammel – conveyor belts and grids which let the smaller pieces of waste fall through. It seems the hamster was small enough to pass through the 150 mm gaps between the shredder blades, but big enough to pass along the trammel without dropping down.'

6 Hamsters are agile and energetic, regularly travelling up to 8 miles during nocturnal hunts for food. Mike – named after one of the crew who found him – is thought to have gone a step too far in his explorations and ended up trapped in a Recyclo-bound white goods skip.

7 Unloaded at the plant, he was whirled in a rotating drum, taken on a conveyor to the shredder, bounced around in a giant sieve and then juddered along a moving grille whose waste disappears into sealed underground sumps. His survival of the 4-minute process comfortably beats the waste-disposal record of Lucky, a hamster from the Anchorage Baptist Temple in Alaska, who only had to deal with a municipal garbage truck.

8 The remotely familiar part of Mike's journey may have been the drum – a giant version of a hamster exercise ball. These have featured in other escapes: a hamster called Roly was found pedalling his along the hard shoulder of the M6 in Birmingham after falling from a car.

9 Pending possible calls from distraught owners, Mike is now getting to know Liam Bull, 10, whose father, Craig, was one of the rescue team. 'He's doing fine now,' said Liam. 'But I can't believe he's still alive after what happened to him.'

Hamster Mike

Questions

?

1 The passage names three hamsters who had dangerous adventures. Using **your own words** as much as possible, explain **briefly** what happened to:

Lucky

___

___

Roly

___

___

Mike

___

___

Read paragraphs 1 to 3. Quote the words or phrases from the passage which tell us:

2 a) that Mike was not badly injured

___

b) that hamsters are sometimes buried when they are not dead

___

c) that you should not send a hamster through the post.

___

Read paragraphs 7 to 9.

3 a) Why does the writer say that the 'rotating drum' in the recycling plant might have been 'familiar' to Mike the hamster?

___

___

b) Why is Mike the hamster now being looked after by Liam Bull?

___

___

Think about the passage as a whole.

4 Did you think this was a good article or not? Explain your answer.

___

___

___

Assessment 4

The Lure of the Bike

1 The bicycle undoubtedly has its downsides. It won't shelter you from the elements, or protect you from the fury of your fellow traveller. It lacks the romance of a sailboat or the simplicity of your own two feet. It will not give you the same sensation that sitting in £180,000-worth of overcharged horsepower does. It is miserable in the wet. No other form of transport ever takes it seriously. It is sliced up by cabs and menaced by buses. It is loathed by motorists and loved by the sort of politicians who would never dream of actually using it. It can't transport you from one end of the world to the other in time for Christmas… It gets stolen, on average, every minute and a half. It delivers you at the end of your journey covered in a light film of sweat and toxic diesel particulates. It requires a lot of silly clothing. And, of course, it is occasionally fatal.

2 And yet cycling obsesses people… Cycling starts to become as much a way of life and a philosophy as it does a form of transport. It spreads from work to weekends to holidays. Cyclists nominate themselves for sponsored rides and charity marathons. They stop thinking in miles and start thinking in kilometres. Almost by mistake, they find themselves in possession of a whole fleet of bikes: one for work, one for speed, one for the wet, one for annoying other people who know about bikes. They realise that one of the major advantages to cycling is the ability – more than that the need – to consume their own bodyweight in spag bol and chocolate cake every day… They arrive at work early every day now, radiant with sweat and self-satisfaction. At home, they talk about getting rid of the car… The thing about it is that it's fun.

3 And so the bicycle – old, cheap, and slightly comic – has become the twenty-first century's great transport success story. Since the millennium, its use in Britain has doubled and doubled again. Thousands now cycle to work, and more take it up every day. It has allowed the reinvention of the British landscape, opening up miles of Forestry Commission land to mountain bikers… It has connected people through events and races and just hanging out. It has become the fastest and most reliable form of transport for people all over the country. In trial after trial, it is the bike which reaches its urban destination faster than the car, the bus, the tube or the pedestrian. Cycling has recycled itself.

Questions

Read paragraph 1.

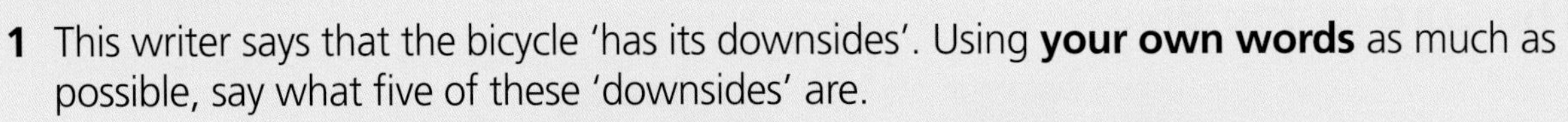

1 This writer says that the bicycle 'has its downsides'. Using **your own words** as much as possible, say what five of these 'downsides' are.

1 ______

2 ______

3 ______

4 ______

5 ______

2 a) The writer uses some negative word choice as she explains these downsides. Quote one negative word or expression that she uses.

______

b) Explain how the word or expression you quoted creates a negative impression.

______

______

Read paragraph 2.

3 The writer says that 'cycling obsesses people'. Using **your own words** as much as possible, give five of the signs that may show someone has become obsessed with cycling.

1 ______

2 ______

3 ______

4 ______

5 ______

4 a) This paragraph contains a number of examples of exaggerated language. Quote one exaggerated word or expression that the writer uses.

______

b) Explain how the word or expression you quoted creates an exaggerated impression.

______

______

Read paragraph 3.

5 The writer says that cycling has become a great 'success story'. Using **your own words** as much as possible, give two pieces of evidence that cycling is a big success.

1 ______________________________

2 ______________________________

6 This extract came from the opening of a book about cycling. Do you think it is a good introduction? Tick one answer.

Yes ☐

No ☐

Give a reason for your answer, supported by evidence from the text.

____

____

Assessment 5

The Drummer Boy

This extract came from a book about Edinburgh's secret underground spaces.

1 One of Edinburgh's most famous underground legends revolves around the discovery of a tunnel in the dungeons of Edinburgh Castle in the early nineteenth century. The City Council was curious to find out where this newly unearthed passage went, but the entrance wasn't large enough to allow exploration – unless the explorer happened to be a particularly small one.

2 Since there were no midgets in the vicinity, the Council decided to send a 10-year-old boy into the tiny aperture to see where the tunnel went to. This may sound like a heartless thing to do, but in those days, thousands of orphans were employed to climb inside chimneys and sweep them – so many Edinburgh children were used to crawling through small, dark spaces. To be fair to the councilmen, they did give the lad a tiny drum – and told him to beat it as he went. That way they could monitor his progress.

3 The child wriggled into the cold, black passage and wormed his way out of sight, frantically beating the drum. As the faint rat-a-tat sound travelled under the High Street, councilmen followed safely along on top, listening to the poor lad's progress. At a spot just short of the Tron Church, the drumming stopped. It did not start up again.

4 Edinburgh Council had a dilemma. Though life was cheap among the city's slum children they couldn't keep sending 10-year-old after 10-year-old into the tunnel – there was no telling how many they might get through. Instead the Council quietly sealed the entrance back up. It was never reopened.

5 Does the tunnel still exist? Did it ever exist? Or is it simply a fairy tale to scare unruly 10-year-olds? Edinburgh Castle is a military garrison and is hardly likely to give away details of a passage running right under its fortifications. But it does seem entirely possible that such a tunnel is real. The Castle was often under siege, and many ancient fortifications used secret passages to sneak messages and important persons through enemy blockades.

6 The legend itself takes many forms. In one popular version it was a bagpiper who was sent underground. This version seems rather dubious – if a burly soldier with a set of pipes could fit into a tunnel there wouldn't be many people who couldn't.

7 And local residents will tell you that on some nights, if there is no traffic around, a faint but frantic drumming can be heard below the streets around the Tron Kirk. In 1994, a woman on a private tour of the underground vaults collapsed after hearing the drummer boy story. When she came to, she told her astonished companions the reason for her fainting fit. She had heard a drumming behind her just before the story was told.

Questions

1 **Read paragraph 1.** The first sentence says Edinburgh has many famous 'underground' legends. Quote three other words from this paragraph that continue the idea of things being 'underground'.

____

____

____

Read paragraphs 1 and 2. Explain **in your own words**:

2 **a)** why the council sent a child, not an adult, down the tunnel

____

____

b) why this did not seem as cruel then as it might seem to us nowadays

____

____

c) why the council members gave the child a drum.

____

____

Read paragraph 3.

3 **a)** Quote two words from this paragraph that show it was difficult for the boy to move inside the tunnel.

____

____

b) Which word makes us feel sympathy for the drummer boy?

____

c) Which word makes us feel annoyed with the councilmen?

____

d) What happened when the boy got to the Tron Church?

____

e) What did this mean had happened to the drummer boy?

____

→

4 **Read paragraph 5.** The paragraph starts with a number of questions. What is the effect of the writer using so many questions together?

____

____

5 Does the writer make you believe that the story of the ghostly drummer boy is true? Tick one answer.

Yes ☐

No ☐

Give a reason for your answer, based on evidence from the text.

____

____

Assessment 6

Komodo Dragons

The following text came from the travel section of a British newspaper.

1 The first Komodo dragon I saw in the wild was a gorgeous adult female, blocking the trail like a two-metre-long **sentinel** in Indonesia's Komodo national park. For a moment, in my **awed** mind, she was a **mythical** dragon demanding payment for passage. But this thought was quickly scuttled as two tourists raced in front to capture a selfie with the apex predator. The **agitated** dragon ran off into the underbrush – they were lucky she didn't run the other way and bite off one of their legs. I'd travelled thousands of miles to see a Komodo dragon and it had just been scared away by **reckless** travellers.

2 Now, a major upgrade of Labuan Bajo regional airport is set to bring more tourists to the 29 islands that make up the park, potentially threatening its famous beast. The airport used to handle 150,000 tourists a year; now it can accommodate 1.5 million, with its new terminal and lengthened runway.

3 The world's largest lizard, the Komodo dragon is arguably Indonesia's best-conserved large animal. Protected under Indonesian law, the population is relatively stable with around 2,500 animals in the park and another 2,000 on larger Flores island, though this population faces habitat loss. Meanwhile, Indonesia's populations of orangutans, tigers, elephants and rhinos continue to plummet as rainforest is destroyed for the palm oil, mining, timber and paper industries.

4 People here truly appreciate the dragon, my guide, Arman Rikardus, told me. He said increasing tourism meant that locals like him didn't have to move to Bali to find work, although they have witnessed a sudden rise in inflation as the number of people moving to Labuan Bajo pushed up the cost of food and housing.

5 He also warned that if tourism gets out of control, the demand for new infrastructure could cut into the dragon's already limited habitat. At present, less than 10% of the national park is actually open to the public, so many of the dragons are able to live out their lives without ever running into a selfie-snapper.

6 The government hopes to mitigate the impact of more tourists: entrance fees for foreigners were recently increased sharply – a day pass with tax now costs between £10 and £15, plus an extra £5 for a guide – in a bid to raise more revenue. The park has also stopped the practice of feeding goats to dragons for tourist entertainment.

7 The local government hopes that tourists will start venturing beyond dragons: Flores is home to several stunning volcanoes, rare birds, and the cave where scientists discovered *homo floresiensis* – Flores man, also known as the hobbit of Indonesia. The region has some of the best diving and snorkelling on the planet. For all that, the Komodo dragon is still the star attraction: outside the new airport sits a massive statue of the area's favourite resident. You can take a selfie with this one without the risk of losing a limb.

Questions

1 **Read paragraph 1.** This paragraph contains a number of words that may be new or unusual for readers. Some of these words have been picked out in **red**. Find the right word in the paragraph to fit each of the meanings given below.

a) from a story or legend

b) careless and foolish

c) a guard or watcher

d) amazed

e) worked up or panicky

2 **Read paragraph 2.** The writer says the airport has had 'a major upgrade'. Using **your own words** as far as possible, give **three** pieces of evidence that prove the airport has been upgraded.

3 **Read paragraph 3.** What does the writer's word choice of 'plummet' tell us about how rainforest destruction is affecting animals in Indonesia?

4 **Read paragraphs 4 and 5.** Using **your own words** as far as possible, explain:

a) one benefit for the islanders of having Komodo dragons there

b) one problem faced by the islanders because the Komodo dragons live there.

5 **Read paragraphs 5 and 6.** Using **your own words** as far as possible, explain three ways that the government has tried to control the impact that tourists have on the park.

6 **Read paragraph 7.**

a) Using **your own words** as far as possible, give three reasons why tourists might want to visit Flores.

b) The writer says that *homo floresiensis* or 'Flores man' is 'also known as the hobbit of Indonesia'. Why do you think it was given this nickname? Choose one answer:

i) Because the discovery had hairy feet

ii) Because J.R.R. Tolkien wrote a book about *homo floresiensis*

iii) Because this person was very small

c) Explain why the last sentence is a good **conclusion** for this newspaper article.

Now think about the whole passage.

7 This passage appeared in the travel section of a newspaper, among articles about places to visit, and holidays that readers could go on. Do you think this is an effective piece of **travel** writing? Give a reason for your answer, supported by evidence from the text.

Assessment 7

NeverSeconds Blogger Nearly Silenced

The following article came from a British newspaper.

Martha Payne — busy campaigning

1 When Martha Payne started posting pictures of her miserable school dinners online, she realised it might ruffle a few feathers.

2 But the 9-year-old never expected her blog to spark a full-scale internet revolt. The young campaigner also could not have predicted the blog's huge popularity would generate more than £60,000 in donations to help feed impoverished children.

3 The saga began 7 weeks ago when Martha, with permission from teachers at Lochgilphead Primary School, started taking pictures of her £2 school dinners and commenting on them as part of a writing project.

4 Her first post included a photo of a measly slice of pizza and a lonely potato croquette, alongside a sprinkling of sweetcorn, a cupcake for dessert and a lot of empty space. Alongside the photo, the schoolgirl wrote: 'The pizza in the first pic was alright but I'd have enjoyed more than one croquette. I'm a growing kid and I need to concentrate all afternoon and I can't do it on one croquette. Do any of you think you could?'

5 Over the next 2 months her daily snaps gathered an impressive following, with more than 2 million people throughout the world logging on and sending in their own pictures for her site.

6 After seeing the photographs, Jamie Oliver, a veteran school food campaigner, sent a tweet to her father, which read: 'Shocking but inspirational blog. Keep going. Big love from Jamie x.'

→

7 However, angry about the headlines Martha's 'NeverSeconds' blog was generating, officials at Argyll and Bute council ordered teachers to stop her from photographing her dinners and rating them online.

8 Last Thursday Martha revealed that teachers wanted her to stop taking the photographs. In a post headed 'Goodbye,' she wrote: 'This morning I got taken out of class by my head teacher and taken to her office. I was told that I could not take any more photos of my school dinners.'

9 In an ill-judged 500-plus word statement, the council accused Martha's blog of being 'misleading'. But the officials seriously underestimated the youngster's internet following and thousands of people, led by Jamie Oliver, took to Twitter to criticise their decision, leading to a humiliating U-turn by the council.

10 Within hours of Oliver tweeting to Martha to 'stay strong' and urging his 2.3 million followers to re-post his message, the schoolgirl's blog became one of the top subjects discussed on the site worldwide. Critics lined up to accuse the council of 'bullying' and thousands signed a petition to get them to overturn the ban.

11 Supporters inundated council phonelines with complaints and also pledged thousands of pounds to the Third World children's charity linked to Martha's blog, smashing her £7,000 target. Donations, from supporters all over the world, including Canada, Germany, America, New Zealand and Australia, now stand at £61,519.07.

12 Council leader Roddy McCuish announced they would be withdrawing the ban with immediate effect. He said: 'It's a good thing to do, to change your mind, and I've certainly done that.'

13 Martha's father, Dave Payne, 39, said common sense had prevailed. 'Martha is beaming,' he said. 'She is delighted she can carry on blogging, but more so about the money being raised for the charity. People have been very, very generous.'

14 Last night the Argyll-based Mary's Meals, the charity supported by Martha's blog, said she had raised enough to build several kitchens for starving children in Malawi. 'Martha's support for Mary's Meals has been amazing and we are extremely grateful for everything that she has done to help us reach some of the hungriest children in the world.'

Questions

1 Read the **headline**. Which technique has the writer used to make this headline memorable? Choose one:

rhyme | simile | alliteration

2 **Read paragraphs 2 and 3.** The writer says Martha Payne 'never expected her blog to spark a full-scale internet revolt'. Explain how we can tell from these paragraphs that Martha did not mean to cause trouble.

3 **Read paragraph 4.** Find **three expressions** in which the writer uses negative word choice to criticise the dinners served at Martha's school.

4 **Read paragraphs 5 and 6.** Using **your own words** as far as possible, give **two** pieces of evidence to prove that the blog soon had 'an impressive following'.

5 **Read paragraph 9.** The writer does not approve of how Argyll and Bute Council acted.

a) Quote one expression from this paragraph that shows the writer's disapproval.

b) Explain how the word(s) you have quoted show the writer's attitude.

6 **Read paragraphs 10 and 11.** Using **your own words** as far as possible, give **three** pieces of evidence that Martha had a lot of support.

7 **Read paragraph 14.** This is the final paragraph of the article. Do you think it is a good ending? Support your answer with evidence from the text.

Think about the passage as a whole.

8 This text is an article from a newspaper. Its purpose is to give information about a story that is new and up-to-date at the time when the story is written. **Read paragraphs 3, 8 and 14.** Quote one expression from one of these paragraphs that shows that the writer was reporting on an up-to-date story when he wrote it. Explain why you chose the expression you have quoted.

Assessment 8

What Milo Saw

Nine-year-old Milo Moon lives with his mother and grandmother. His grandmother is beginning to forget things and finding life more difficult. After she accidentally causes a fire in their house, they realise that it is time to find an old people's home for Gran to live in.

1 A week later, Milo buckled Gran into the back seat of the car and climbed in beside her.

2 'Not in the back, Milo,' said Mum. 'I need you up front to operate the machine.' She waved her hand at the satnav clamped to the windscreen. Milo tried to exchange a look with Gran, but Gran wasn't paying attention. She sat with her hands folded in her lap, staring out of the window.

3 She'd had that same empty look when Milo went up to her room earlier to help her get dressed. *You'll be back for Christmas*, he'd promised her as he pulled her pop socks over her calves. But she'd just gazed down at the lines in her palms.

4 When he went back downstairs he didn't tell Mum that there was a wet patch on the carpet because Gran had left the tap running.

5 Milo didn't tell Mum half the things he knew about Gran.

6 Like that she'd get up in the middle of the night and come into his room and say that she was going on her honeymoon to Greece and that Great-Gramps was waiting for her.

7 Or that she sometimes got the shakes so bad he was worried she'd keel over and bang her head on the corner of the dresser and knock herself out.

8 Milo typed in the postcode of the first nursing home on his list. Then he snuck his arm past the gear stick and the handbrake and put his hand on Gran's.

9 Her wrinkly fingers tremored under his.

10 Mum narrowly missed crashing into the old Volvo parked outside Mr Overend's house. 'That stupid car, taking up all that space and never getting used. Someone should take it to the scrap yard.'

11 As Milo looked up he saw a fuzzy shadow leaning into Mr Overend's bedroom window. He wondered how long it had been since Mr Overend got behind the wheel of his car – in fact he wondered how long it had been since Mr Overend had last left his house.

12 As Milo shifted his head and focused in on the images through the small 'O' of his vision, he felt kind of lucky that he didn't have to see it all. At least he only got a bit of the grey sky and the grey pavements and the grey leafless trees. People who saw everything at once must feel drowned by the world. All Milo had to do was to move his head and focus on something else and pretend the bad bits weren't there.

13 He remembered that day in January when he'd sat in Dr Nolan's examination room. He'd liked the feel of the big chair with the tall headrest and all those machines that made his eyes go funny. The room was underground so it didn't have any windows. There were posters all over the walls of what eyes looked like from the inside: as Dr Nolan explained what was wrong with Milo's eyes he'd pointed to the nerves and veins and muscles, like a map of the London Underground only messier. And then he'd shown Milo the picture of an orange moon and said that was what his retina looked like, that the lighter bits of orange were the reason why he could only see part of the world, the bit through the pinhole. That's when Mum had started crying, which meant Dr Nolan had to get some tissues from the loo, but Milo hadn't been able to stop staring at that orange moon. It was beautiful.

Questions

1 **Read paragraph 1.** Which expression shows that we have begun reading part of the way through a story? Explain how the expression you have quoted shows this.

2 **Read paragraphs 2 and 3.** Using **your own words** as far as possible, give evidence:

a) that Gran needs Milo

b) that Mum needs Milo.

3 **Read paragraphs 4 to 7.** Explain three things that Milo knows about Gran but has not told to Mum. Use **your own words**.

4 **Read paragraphs 8 and 9.**

a) What does the word 'snuck' tell us about the way Milo took hold of Gran's hand?

b) What does the word 'tremored' tell us about Gran?

5 **Read paragraph 12.**

a) Find an example of repetition used in this paragraph.

b) What effect does the author create by repeating this word?

6 **Read paragraph 13.** We already know that Gran has problems. Now we learn that Milo has a problem too. Using **your own words** as far as possible, explain what Milo's problem is.

Assessment 9

Arriving in Edinburgh

The American writer Bill Bryson is touring Britain and arrives in Edinburgh. Local readers would be able to tell that he is a tourist – in the city, what Bryson calls the 'Memorial' *is always referred to as the Scott* Monument.

1 And so I went to Edinburgh. Can there anywhere be a more beautiful and beguiling city to arrive at by train early on a crisp, dark November evening? To emerge from the bustling subterranean bowels of Waverley Station and find yourself in the very heart of such a glorious city is a happy experience indeed. I hadn't been to Edinburgh for years and had forgotten just how captivating it can be. Every monument was lit with golden floodlights – the castle and Bank of Scotland headquarters on the hill, the Balmoral Hotel and the Scott Memorial down below – which gave them a certain eerie grandeur. The city was abustle with end-of-day activity. Buses swept through Princes Street and shop and office workers scurried along the pavements, hastening home to have their haggis and cock-a-leekie soup and indulge in a few skirls or whatever it is Scots do when the sun goes down.

2 I'd booked a room in the Caledonian Hotel, which was a rash and extravagant thing to do, but it's a terrific building and an Edinburgh institution and I just had to be part of it for one night, so I set off down Princes Street, past the Gothic rocket ship of the Scot Memorial.

3 Edinburgh felt like a different country. The buildings were thin and tall in an un-English fashion, the money was different, even the air and light felt different in some ineffable northern way. Every bookshop window was full of books about Scotland or by Scottish authors. And of course the voices were different. I walked along, feeling as if I had left England far behind, and then I would pass something familiar and think, 'Oh look, they have Marks and Spencer here,' as if I were in Reykjavik or Stavanger and oughtn't to expect to find British things. It was most refreshing.

→

4 I checked in to the Caledonian, dumped my things in the room, and immediately returned to the streets, eager to be out in the open air and to take in whatever Edinburgh had to offer. I trudged up a long, curving back hill to the castle, but the grounds were shut for the night, so I contented myself with a shuffling amble down the Royal Mile, which was nearly empty of life and very handsome in a dour, Scottish sort of way. I passed the time browsing in the windows of the many tourist shops that stand along it, reflecting on what a lot of things the Scots have given the world – kilts, bagpipes, tam-o'-shanters, tins of oatcakes, bright yellow jumpers with big diamond patterns, plaster casts of Greyfriars Bobby looking soulful, sacks of haggis – and how little anyone but a Scot would want them.

5 At the bottom of the Royal Mile, I came up against the entrance to the Palace of Holyroodhouse, and picked my way back to the centre of things along a series of darkened back lanes. Eventually I ended up in an unusual pub on St Andrews Square called Tiles – an apt name since every inch of it from floor to ceiling was covered in elaborate, chunky, Victorian tiles. In any case, something about it must have appealed to me, because I drank a foolish amount of beer and emerged to find that nearly all the restaurants roundabout were closed, so I toddled back to my hotel, where I winked at the night staff and put myself to bed.

Questions

1 Read paragraph 1.

a) Quote **four** separate expressions Bill Bryson uses to praise Edinburgh.

b) Read the final sentence. Explain how we can tell from this sentence that the writer is not Scottish.

2 Read paragraph 2. Explain, using **your own words**:

a) one reason why the writer felt he **should not** have checked in to the Caledonian Hotel

b) one reason why the writer felt he **should** check in to the Caledonian Hotel.

3 Read paragraph 3. The writer says 'Edinburgh felt like a different country.' Using **your own words** as far as possible, list four things that made Edinburgh feel different.

4 Read paragraph 4.

a) Quote **two** separate expressions that show Bill Bryson did not spend long in the hotel room.

b) Explain how **one** of the expressions that you have quoted shows us this.

5 Read paragraphs 4 and 5. The writer uses a number of different expressions to suggest different ways in which he walked around Edinburgh.

a) Quote **one** of the expressions he uses.

b) Explain what this word suggests about the way in which the writer was walking.

Now think about the passage as a whole.

6 Which genre of writing is this? Choose one:

fiction OR non-fiction

Give a reason for your answer, based on evidence from the text.

7 Does the text make you want to visit Edinburgh? Explain your answer by referring to details from the text.

Assessment 10

The Streak

1 It started on a train. I am sure of it. The 3,218-night reading marathon that my father and I call The Streak started on a train to Boston, when I was in third grade. We were reading L. Frank Baum's *The Tin Woodsman of Oz*, the twelfth book in the beloved Oz series, a few hours into our trip. The woman across the aisle turned to us and asked why my father was reading to me on a train. We simply told her that this was what we always did – he had been reading to me every night for as long as I could remember, ever since we read *Pinocchio* when I was four. Being on vacation didn't make much of a difference. Why not read? Why not always read?

2 But her surprise made us think. If we were going to read on vacation anyway, how hard could it be to make reading every night an official goal? I suggested to my father that we aim for one hundred consecutive nights of reading, and he agreed to the challenge. This is how I remember it.

3 If you ask my father though, as many people recently have, he'll paint an entirely different picture.

4 'We were on the train to Boston, and the woman next to us said how sweet it was that I was reading to you. I told her right away that we were on a streak, forty nights in! I was pleased with myself, absurdly pleased with myself, pleased as a peacock to have made it forty nights.'

5 The thing is, no matter how many times we are asked, we can never get this story straight. We agree on a few of the details, but I was very young and he is getting older. Some memories blend together with others, and our individual versions of how The Streak started change so often, it is nearly impossible to come to any sort of agreement. We can't even remember when we started calling it The Streak, or whose idea it was to do so. If we knew it would eventually reach over thirty-two hundred nights and span almost nine years, from elementary school to my first day of college, we might have taken notes in the beginning. Years passed before we even started keeping track of the books we read.

➜

6 Just because we didn't know how it would end, though, didn't mean we took our Streak lightly. Our rules were always clear and firm: we had to read for at least 10 minutes (but almost always much more) per night, every night, with no exception. It should come from whatever book we were reading at the time, but if we were out of the house when midnight approached, anything from magazines to baseball programs would do. The reading should be done in person but, if the opportunity wasn't there, over the phone would suffice. Well, just barely. I could always hear the annoyance in my father's voice when I called to inform him that I was sleeping at a friend's. He'd sigh and pout down the phone, and I'd wait for him to go get our book.

7 We remember details from later in The Streak better, both because they are more recent, and because our record was becoming more impressive. Once we reached over a thousand nights, close calls and readings at quarter to midnight became more nail-biting issues. Of course we both remember how it eventually ended. That's the sort of event even my father can't forget, an event we dreaded for years. To get there though, we need a beginning, and frankly I don't know what that beginning is.

Questions

1 Read paragraph 1.

a) Identify one technique the writer uses that makes her sound very certain about how The Streak began.

b) The writer says that the 'reading marathon' she shared with her father began on a train journey. Quote the words from this paragraph that tell us The Streak had actually already begun before this journey.

2 Read paragraphs 3 and 4.

a) The writer says her father will 'paint an entirely different picture'. What figure of speech is this? Choose one:

simile OR metaphor OR symbol

b) The writer's father says he felt 'pleased as a peacock'. What figure of speech is this? Choose one:

simile OR metaphor OR symbol

c) Quote the sentence which shows that her father thinks The Streak began before the night of the train journey.

3 Read paragraph 5. Give three reasons why the writer and her father 'can never get this story straight'. Use **your own words**.

4 Read paragraph 6. The writer says 'Our rules were always clear and firm'. However, each rule is sometimes bent or broken. Using **your own words** as far as possible, say what the rules were, and how they could be broken. The first one has been done for you as an example.

Rule 1: *Each night's reading must be not less than 10 minutes.*

BUT: *They nearly always read for much longer than that.*

Once you have read the example, explain rules 2 and 3 in the same way.

5 Read paragraph 7.

a) Give **two** reasons, using **your own words** as far as possible, why the writer and her father 'remember details from later in The Streak better'.

b) The writer says they both 'remember how it eventually ended'. By referring back to a detail from paragraph 5, explain what brought the reading Streak to an end.

Think about the passage as a whole.

6 Do you think the writer has given you a clear explanation of what The Reading Streak was? Give a reason for your answer, using evidence from the text.

Assessment 11

The Mystery of the Clockwork Sparrow

This is the beginning of a novel set in London in around 1909. Sophie is on her way to begin work in a new job.

1 Sophie hung on tightly to the leather strap as the omnibus rattled forwards. Another Monday morning and, all about her, London was whirring into life: damp and steamy with last night's rain and this morning's smoke. As she stood between a couple of clerks wearing bowler hats and carrying newspapers, she gazed out of the window at the grey street, wondering whether the faint fragrance of spring she'd caught on the wind had been just her imagination. She found herself thinking about the garden of Orchard House: the daffodils that must be blooming there now, the damp earth and the smell of rain in the grass.

2 'Piccadilly Circus!' yelled the conductor as the omnibus clattered to a halt, and Sophie pushed her thoughts away. She straightened her hat, grasped her umbrella in a neatly-gloved hand, and slipped between the clerks and past an elderly lady who said, 'Dear me!' as if quite scandalised at the thought of a young lady alone, recklessly jumping on and off omnibuses. Sophie paid no attention and hopped down onto the pavement. There was simply no sense in listening. After all, she wasn't that sort of young lady any more.

3 As the omnibus drew away, she turned and gazed for a moment at the enormous white building that towered above her. Sinclair's department store was so new that, as yet, it had not even opened its doors to customers. But already it was the most famous store in London – and therefore, some said, the whole world. With its magnificent columns and ranks of coloured flags, it wasn't like any other shop Sophie had ever seen. It was more like a classical temple that had sprung up, white and immaculate against the smog and dirt of Piccadilly. The huge plate-glass windows were shrouded with royal-blue silk curtains, making it look like the stage in a grand theatre before the performance has begun.

4 The owner of Sinclair's department store was Mr Edward Sinclair, who was as famous as the store itself. He was an American, a self-made man, renowned for his elegance, for the single, perfect orchid he always wore in his buttonhole, for the ever-changing string of beautiful ladies on his arm, and, most of all, for his wealth. Although they had only been working for him for a few weeks, and most of them had barely set eyes on him, the staff of Sinclair's had taken to referring to him as 'the Captain' because rumour had it that he

had run away to sea in his youth. There were already a great number of rumours about Edward Sinclair. But, whether the stories were true or not, it seemed an apt nickname. After all, the store itself was a little like a ship: as glittering and luxurious as an ocean liner ready to carry its customers proudly on a journey to an exotic new land.

5 Through the doors was another world. The staff corridors were humming with activity. All about her, people were hurrying about carrying palms in pots, or stepladders and tins of paint, or stacks of the distinctive royal-blue and gold Sinclair's boxes. A smart saleswoman whisked by with an exquisitely beaded evening gown draped carefully over her arm; another hustled along with an armful of parasols, seemingly in a terrific rush; and the strict store manager, Mr Cooper, could be seen dressing down a salesman about the condition of his gloves. Sophie dived in among them and then slipped into the empty cloakroom to take off her coat and hat.

6 It seemed extraordinary that she was here at all. Even a year ago, the thought of earning her own living would never have entered her imagination – and now, here she was, a fully-fledged shop girl. She paused for a moment before the cloakroom looking-glass to survey her hair, and pushed a hairpin back into place. Mr Cooper was a stickler for immaculate personal appearances, but, worse than that, she knew that Edith and the other girls would be only too quick to notice any shortcomings. Once upon a time she had been rather vain about her looks, carefully brushing her hair one hundred times each night, and fussing Miss Pennyfeather to tie her velvet ribbon in exactly the right sort of bow, but now she only wanted to look neat and business-like. She didn't feel in the least like the girl she had been back then. Her face in the looking glass was familiar, but strange: she looked older somehow, pale and tired and out of sorts.

Questions

1 **Read paragraphs 1 and 2.**

a) Identify **one** detail the writer uses in paragraph 1 or 2 to make London sound unpleasant. Explain how the detail you have chosen creates this effect.

b) Identify **one** detail the writer uses in paragraph 1 or 2 to show that the story is set more than 100 years ago. Explain how the detail you have chosen creates this effect.

2 **Read paragraph 3.** Explain how the writer creates a contrast between the Sinclair's building and Piccadilly.

3 **Read paragraph 4.**

a) Using **your own words** explain **three** things Mr Edward Sinclair is renowned for.

b) Using **your own words** explain **two** ways that the writer makes Sinclair seem mysterious.

4 **Read paragraph 5.**

a) Identify **one** technique the writer uses to suggest speed or busyness. Explain how the technique you have chosen creates this effect.

b) Mr Cooper is said to be 'dressing down' one of the salesmen. What does this mean? Choose **one** answer.

i) Mr Cooper is telling the salesman what to wear.

ii) Mr Cooper is giving the salesman a telling off.

iii) Mr Cooper is taking the salesman's shop uniform away and firing him from his job.

5 **Read paragraph 6.** The writer is trying to intrigue her readers and make them want to keep reading. Pick **one** detail we learn about Sophie in this paragraph and explain how it might make the audience read on.

Think about the text as a whole.

6 The purpose of this text is to start off a much longer novel. Explain one way in which the writer shows that she is beginning a much longer story.

Assessment 12

Blame My Brain

The following extract comes from a book about the science of how teenage brains work.

1 For a long time, people have assumed that the inability to get out of bed is just teenagers being lazy. We have blamed it on the fact that they choose to stay up too late and therefore can't get up in the morning. But new research shows that laziness and deliberately late nights are not entirely to blame. It's the special teenage brain kicking in.

2 Circadian rhythms are the patterns of sleeping and waking, which all animals have. The brain region which seems most important in controlling these rhythms is deep within a part of the brain called the hypothalamus. We call the cells that control our waking patterns the biological or body clock.

3 In a normal and fully developed adult human brain, the body clock is 'on' for about 16 hours a day, generally corresponding to daylight, and during this time we tend to be awake. In fact, it's quite difficult to sleep while the brain is like that.

4 Then the body clock switches off, usually responding to daylight disappearing, for around 8 hours, and we tend to feel sleepy during that time. In fact, it is hard to stay awake, unless we have a sleep problem or have something keeping us awake, like caffeine, or a party, or worry.

5 But teenagers are much more interesting than that, of course. Suddenly, around puberty, the body clock seems to work differently. Research shows that teenagers (and this is true until the early 20s) need around 9¼ hours of sleep a night. You don't need to be a maths genius to work out that if you don't go to sleep till midnight, you are a long way from being ready to wake up when your parents attempt to rouse you at seven. Your brain won't be ready till past nine.

6 By being forced to get up after only 7 hours instead of 9, you are building up a sleep loss of 10 hours during every school week. According to sleep expert Mary Carskadon, teenagers are getting on average 7½ hours of sleep on school nights. And a quarter are getting only 6½.

7 Another problem with being woken too early is that you'll also be losing a special sort of sleep – REM sleep. REM stands for 'rapid eye movement' because when you are in it your eyelids will be fluttering. REM sleep tends to happen at certain stages during your sleep cycle and is a particularly deep sleep. It is during this time that you dream. Experts now believe that REM sleep is particularly important for memory and learning.

8 So? Can't you just lie in at the weekend? Isn't that what weekends are for?

9 Unfortunately, life is not so simple. Although you can make up some sleep at weekends, this doesn't help your body clock and may actually disrupt it further. There is no doubt that, even with extra sleep at the weekends, very many adolescents show symptoms of severe sleep deprivation.

10 Even though you can't stop having a teenage brain – and why would you want to? – there are things you can do to help yourself get the sleep you need when you need. You can minimise the effects of the sleep deprivation that cruel adults and the modern world force on you. You still won't find that your brain does your history homework in your sleep, but you might even find that you have the energy to do it yourself.

- Bright light in the morning is the best way to tell your body clock to wake up. It may sound unpleasant, but if someone opens your curtains and switches on all the lights before you need to get up, this will help.
- From lunchtime onwards, avoid coffee, tea, Coke with caffeine in, and tobacco (avoid tobacco altogether, in fact – but you know that).
- If you are sleepy during certain times of day, try to use those moments for active, stimulating things so you avoid falling asleep, therefore keeping your body clock on cue for sleeping at night.
- Do try to catch up at weekends – by trying to go to sleep at a sensible time on at least one of the nights, rather than by sleeping in till lunchtime, which will not help your body clock.
- Try to help your body clock by getting lots of light through the morning and darkness in the evening. During the day, the more you can be outside, the more natural light you will get, helping your body clock.
- If getting to sleep is your problem, it is even more important not to compensate by sleeping late in the morning.
- A warm milky drink (not coffee or tea) can help.
- Do not take sleeping pills to help you sleep unless a doctor prescribes them.

Questions

1 **Read paragraph 1**. Explain, using **your own words** as far as possible:

a) what people **used to think** was the reason why teenagers could not get out of bed

b) what people **now think** is the reason why teenagers are not good at getting out of bed.

2 **Read paragraph 2.** The writer bases her book on lots of scientific research and knowledge. Identify **one** example of scientific word choice or jargon that she uses in this paragraph.

3 **Read paragraphs 3 to 5.** The writer explains the difference between how adult brains work, and how teenage brains work. Explain, using **your own words** as far as possible:

a) how adult brains behave during daylight

b) how adult brains behave during the hours of darkness

c) how teenage brains are different.

4 **Read paragraphs 6 and 7.**

a) Using **your own words**, explain **two** key sleep problems that teenagers experience.

b) The writer refers to someone called Mary Carskadon. Explain one way in which she makes Carskadon's information seem convincing.

5 **Read paragraph 8.**

a) What technique does the writer repeatedly use here?

b) What effect does she create by using this technique?

6 **Read paragraph 10, including the list of bullet points.** Using **your own words** as far as possible, find **three** things the writer says you **should** do, and **three** things she says you **should not** do 'to help yourself get the sleep you need'. You should organise your answer as two lists. The first answer in each list has been done for you as an example:

DO tell yourself to wake up by filling your bedroom with light.

Now add three more DOs to the list.

DON'T smoke or have caffeinated drinks in the afternoon or evening.

Now add three more DON'Ts to your list.

Assessments 13, 14 and 15

So far, the practice assessments have asked you questions, or given you small tasks to do, such as identifying a technique or giving an explanation. If you are trying to pass the Reading unit tests in English at National 3 and beyond, the questions will ask you something, or tell you what to do. If you go on to further English studies, your close reading skills will be assessed in the National exams, as well as in the unit tests for these courses. In these exams, each question is followed by a number. For example:

1 What are some of the advantages for companies who hire members of staff with autism? Refer to paragraph 10 in your answer, **using your own words.** **4**

2 **In your own words**, explain in what ways 'there is a lot of ground to make up' for people with autism in the workplace. Give evidence from paragraph 11 to support your answer. **3**

What do you think the number in bold at the end of the question is for? Stop and think. You might want to discuss this with a partner before you share your answer with the rest of the class.

Did you work it out? The number at the end of the question gives you a hint about how much work you have to do in your answer. So, in question 1 above, the marker is looking for pupils to find four advantages. In question 2, the marker will be hoping that pupils can give three pieces of evidence. For both of these questions, the marker would also be very happy if the pupil organised his or her answers by writing them as numbered or bullet-pointed lists.

Some questions you will meet will be worth 2 marks. That might mean you should give two small details, or perhaps a detail from the text followed by a comment or explanation. Or you might be able to earn two marks for a detailed explanation, and one mark for a simpler explanation.

However many marks are available, the wording of the question will also, of course, give you guidance about what you need to do to write a good answer.

Assessments 13, 14 and 15 will tell you, at the end of each question, how many marks are available for your answer. Assessment 13 will also give you some hints about how to answer. By the time you get on to assessments 14 and 15, you should be able to work out for yourself how to tackle and organise your answers. Although intentionally harder than those in the previous pages, assessments 13, 14, and 15 are not structured and worded exactly like the National exams, nor do they show the exact mark allocation, but they will nonetheless help you to develop the skills you will need.

Assessment 13

Made in Scotland: A History of Invention

This text came from the BBC iWonder website, which aims to give thought-provoking answers to fascinating questions.

About 1100: the birth of golf

One of Scotland's first inventions was golf. It is now a global sport with over 32,000 courses across the world.

Although the Netherlands has laid claim to golf, the modern 18-hole game began in Scotland. The earliest known games were most likely played around the year 1100 on the Scottish east coast where shepherds used sticks to hit pebbles into rabbit holes. Over the next two centuries, the game's popularity grew in Scotland. In the sixteenth century golf evolved, with different clubs being used to hit the balls into holes marked by flags. In 1744, the oldest surviving rules of golf were drafted in Edinburgh.

1614: John Napier and logarithms

In the seventeenth century John Napier laid the foundations for modern computing when he invented logarithms.

Napier first presented the concept of logarithms in 1614. Put simply, a logarithm answers the question: how many of one number do we multiply to get another number? For example, we need to multiply 2 three times to get 8: $2 \times 2 \times 2 = 8$. So the logarithm is three. The applications were widespread: seafarers could chart their position accurately and astronomers were able to calculate the orbits of planets. Today, computers have replaced written tables, but the principle remains the same.

1765: James Watt's improved steam engine

In the eighteenth century, Scotland was full of leaders in science and philosophy. One was James Watt, who invented a new type of steam engine.

James Watt was working as an instrument maker at Glasgow University when he was given a Newcomen steam engine to fix. Thomas Newcomen invented the first steam engine around 1712, but Watt believed he could improve it. Watt's masterstroke came in 1765 when he thought of a way to stop the steam escaping, increasing the engine's efficiency threefold. In mines, mills and factories, the steam engine transformed the way people worked.

1800: the first professional police force

The steam revolution was bringing increasing numbers into Britain's cities. The need for law and order was key.

In June 1800, the British parliament passed the Glasgow Police Act, establishing the City of Glasgow Police, Britain's first professional police force. In addition to policing, the duties of this fledgling force included fire-fighting, street sweeping and calling the time. It ran from 1800 to 1975 and was then amalgamated into Strathclyde Police.

→

1847: James Young Simpson and anaesthetic

While Napier and Watt made navigation and transport much easier, Scots were committed to improving and saving lives in other branches of science.

As a medical student, James Young Simpson was horrified at the sight of operations performed without anaesthetics. After becoming Professor of Midwifery at Edinburgh University in 1840, he attempted to find a drug that would block his patients' pain. Eventually he came across a liquid called chloroform. After successfully testing it on himself and two assistants, Simpson realised its potential. He revolutionised childbirth, making it much safer.

1875: Alexander Graham Bell and the telephone

Today, with nearly 7 billion mobile phones worldwide, there can be no doubt as to the significance of Alexander Graham Bell's invention.

Edinburgh-born Alexander Graham Bell was fascinated with speech and our ability to hear. This led to him experimenting with ways of transmitting sound electronically. By 1875, now living in Canada, he had developed a receiver that turned electricity into sound. Famously, Bell's first phone communication was to his assistant in another room: 'Mr Watson, come here, I want to see you.' Although others were researching along similar lines, Bell was the first to patent his design in 1876.

1926: John Logie Baird and television

Television is perhaps the twentieth century's most influential invention.

Helensburgh-born John Logie Baird was an inventor to his fingertips. Before television he had even invented a thermal undersock, used by soldiers during the First World War. His first mechanical television was a primitive affair whose parts included a tea chest and bicycle lights. Despite this, Baird successfully demonstrated his television in early 1926, even though the crude picture was at a resolution of barely 30 lines. But from these first small steps, television would go on to change the world.

➜

1997: Dolly the sheep

One pioneering Scottish scientific achievement announced in 1997 means we can now create copies of living things.

Dolly the sheep is the world's most famous clone. She was created from an adult sheep cell at the Roslin Institute, now part of Edinburgh University, and born in 1996. Dolly was cloned to allow research into genetic diseases for which there is currently no cure, but ethical questions arising from her cloning have sparked much debate. Dolly is just one of the many ground-breaking innovations that place one small nation at the forefront of inventions that have shaped the modern world.

Questions

?

1 **Read the section about the birth of golf**. The writer mentions **three** important steps in the evolution of golf. Using **your own words**, say when each of these stages happened, and what happened at that point. **3**

HINT: write your answer as a list. Start each item on your list with a date.

2 **Read the section about Napier and logarithms.** Using **your own words** as far as possible, explain why logarithms were important when they were first invented, and why they are still important to us now. **3**

3 **Read the section about James Watt's steam engine.** Using **your own words** as far as possible, explain how we know that Watt's improvements to the engine made a significant difference. **2**

HINT: you will get 1 mark if you give a brief or simple explanation, but you can earn the full 2 marks for a more detailed and developed answer.

4 **Read the section about the Glasgow Police.**

a) The author says this was the 'first professional police force'. Quote an expression which continues the idea of this being the 'first' force and explain how it does so. **2**

HINT: you will get 1 mark for quoting a suitable expression, and 1 mark for your explanation.

b) Identify one duty carried out by the City of Glasgow Police that you find surprising, and explain why you are surprised by it. **2**

HINT: you will get 1 mark for identifying a surprising duty, and 1 mark for your explanation.

5 **Read the section about James Young Simpson.**

a) Explain in **your own words** what 'horrified' Simpson. **2**

HINT: you will get 1 mark if you give a brief or simple explanation, but you can earn the full 2 marks for a more detailed and developed answer.

b) Identify an expression which tells us that Simpson's discovery had a major impact, and explain how it does so. **2**

HINT: you will get 1 mark for quoting a suitable expression, and 1 mark for your explanation.

6 **Read the section about Alexander Graham Bell.** How does this particular invention not quite fit the title of the whole passage? **2**

HINT: you will get 1 mark if you give a brief or simple explanation, but you can earn the full 2 marks for a more detailed and developed answer.

7 **Read the section about John Logie Baird.** What evidence is there that the first television was 'a primitive affair'? **2**

HINT: give two clear separate details in your answer.

8 **Read the section about Dolly the sheep**. The writer uses a number of expressions that tell us Scotland is often the first country to create something new. Identify **three** of these. **3**

Assessment 14

Message in a Bottle

The following article appeared in the travel section of a national newspaper.

1 I was 22 and on a family holiday in the Turks and Caicos Islands when it first happened. My dad and I had got a boat to an uninhabited island only for rain to start pelting down the moment we arrived. As we strode along the beach, I saw a glint of blue glass on the shoreline. I realised it was a wine bottle – and that there was something inside it. A jolt of excitement ran through me.

2 I'd always dreamed of finding a message in a bottle and my hands were shaking as I uncorked it. It turned out the bottle had been dropped 8 months previously, in October 2006, by a couple on board a cruise from the Portuguese island of Madeira. It wasn't a treasure map or a cry for help but, to me, it was a miracle. The bottle had survived its journey across the Atlantic and I'd found it.

3 I emailed the senders as soon as I got back to the hotel. They were happy to know someone had got their message, but perhaps were disappointed it had been found so soon after they'd dropped it overboard. For me, however, it was a profound experience. It sparked a sort of obsession and I started spending every spare cent and every spare moment looking for more bottles. My family and I had always beach-combed for shells on vacation and when you figure out the knack of looking, you start finding more. I figured – crazy as it sounds – that I could do the same with messages in bottles.

4 Since that holiday, 8 years ago, I've found more than 80 messages in bottles, mostly on the Turks and Caicos, which oceanographer Curtis Ebbesmeyer calls a 'flotsam* magnet'. Bottles have been washing up on the islands since at least the 1800s; the Turks and Caicos National Museum features a large collection that belonged to its late founder. I've picked up bottles from senders in the US, Canada, Britain, France, Germany, Spain, the Philippines, Puerto Rico and Switzerland. It's not just messages either. I've found artwork, business cards, dollar bills … even a crumbling piece of wedding cake.

→

* flotsam – items floating in the sea that eventually wash up on the shore

5 I try to make contact with the senders if I can. The internet has made that easier than it would have been in the past and I often get help through my blog – *Message In A Bottle Hunter* – and Facebook page. I travelled to Düsseldorf last summer to meet Sabine Roy, a German travel agent whose message I found back in 2011, and Thorston Falke, the man who put the two of us in touch. Sabine's message had deteriorated badly by the time I'd found it; all I could make out was a cruise ship letterhead, her name and 'Düsseldorf'. I tried tracing her for 4 years before I thought of posting a call-out on social media. Within a day Thorston had tracked her down.

6 It's almost like going on a blind date when I meet a sender. We've been brought together entirely by chance and there are no guarantees we'll have anything in common. I guess it could be awkward but that hasn't been my experience so far. People who send messages in bottles tend to be adventurous types and are often as excited to meet up as I am.

7 British folks are especially welcoming. When I told one sender, Kevin Euridge, I was heading to Europe, he invited me to spend a couple of nights at his place in Kent. We hiked from his back garden all the way to Canterbury Cathedral. To walk through land I'd only read about when studying Chaucer as an English major, that was incredible to me. Meeting people this way allows me to see and engage with places in ways I'd never experience under other circumstances.

8 Sometimes I'm too late. One of the oldest messages I found was in a Coca-Cola bottle from the 1970s. It was from a woman called Tina who said she was the owner of the Beachcomber motel in New Hampshire. She offered a $150 reward for the bottle's return. I did a lot of detective work; I went through the local chamber of commerce, I contacted the tax assessor to figure out who owned the land. I eventually found out Tina had died but I met her daughter, who was astonished when I showed her the message her mother had sent decades before.

9 A lot of people forget they have sent these messages and when you present them with these pieces of their past, it's almost like time travel. Sometimes it's funny, like when I found a note from a guy who claimed he had been taken prisoner 'by a grumpy old man' and gave his coordinates and his mother's address in Baltimore. When I called her, she told me her son must have sent the bottle while on a boat trip with his dad in the 1990s. At other times, it's moving. In 2008, I found a bottle containing a message from a woman called Janet. She had dropped it in the Delaware river in 1981 to commemorate her marriage and it had made its way to the Atlantic where it spent 27 years bobbing about. When I made contact with her and read her message down the phone to her, she started crying. The couple had divorced a few years previously and the message took her straight back to a time when they had imagined they would be together forever.

10 I can't see myself giving up my hunt anytime soon – I'm hooked on the pure adventure of it all. Although I now know more about oceanography and currents than when I started, you never know where bottles will wash up, so every find is still a treasure. On a deeper level, I guess it's about finding connection. There's such a business in fear these days but when someone tosses a bottle into the sea it's in the hope that someone they have never met, in a place they may never have visited, might one day find it and say hi. That's beautiful to me.

Questions

?

1 **Read paragraphs 1 and 2.** Identify an expression that shows the writer's 'excitement' and explain how it does so. **2**

2 **Read paragraph 3.**

a) Using **your own words**, give evidence that finding more bottles became an 'obsession' for the writer. **2**

b) Using **your own words**, explain why the writer believed he would be able to find more bottles. **2**

3 **Read paragraph 4.** The Turks and Caicos are described as 'a flotsam magnet'.

a) Identify the figure of speech used in this expression. **1**

b) Using **your own words**, list the evidence that shows these islands are indeed 'a flotsam magnet'. **4**

4 **Read paragraph 5**. The writer says that the internet has made searching for senders 'easier'. Using **your own words** as far as possible, explain how the story he tells in this paragraph proves that this is true. **2**

5 **Read paragraph 6.** The writer says that meeting senders is 'almost like going on a blind date'.

a) Identify the figure of speech used in this expression. **1**

b) Using **your own words**, explain how meeting senders is indeed 'almost like going on a blind date'. **2**

6 **Read paragraphs 7 and 8.** In **your own words**, explain how the writer illustrates the idea:

a) that British people are 'especially welcoming' **2**

b) that he sometimes arrives 'too late'. **2**

7 **Read paragraph 9**. In **your own words**, explain:

a) what makes the first story 'funny' **2**

b) what makes the second story 'moving'. **2**

8 **Read paragraph 10.** Identify an expression that shows that the bottles the writer finds are important to him. Explain how the expression you have quoted creates this effect. **2**

Assessment 15

The Blood Bikers

The following passage came from a national newspaper.

A blood biker

1 As Nigel sits in his kitchen late on a Wednesday night and pours himself another coffee, his phone vibrates. He looks at the text message: *'Urgent blood sample from Kettering to Birmingham.'* 'Right,' he says. 'We're off.' He downs the contents of his cup, grabs his leather riding gloves and leads me outside to his motorbike. We climb on and ride away into the cold night.

2 Nigel isn't heading out on a pleasure trip: although he's not paid for it, his mission is deadly serious. Their name might sound a bit ominous, but the 1,500-strong gang he belongs to is a long way from the Hell's Angels. They're called the blood bikers: men and women all over Britain who dedicate a few evenings a week to transporting hospital deliveries across the country as stand-ins for the daytime professionals. They are all volunteers, and in 2013 they responded to around 35,000 urgent requests from hospitals, saving the NHS hundreds of thousands of pounds. They take everything from blood and platelets to medicine and breast milk.

3 Nigel's first stop is Kettering General hospital, about 60 miles from his home. As usual, he is in a hurry – the blood sample is needed for a patient early the next morning. In situations like this, the work of the blood bikers is essential: without it, urgently needed medical supplies would far more often be stuck in traffic.

4 But despite the rush, and despite the fact that they are provided with blue lights and sirens, Nigel and his fellow bikers have to stick scrupulously to the speed limit and stop at every red light. (MI6, bomb disposal units and the coastguard operate under the same strictures.) As a result the blue lights are of limited use.

5 From the darkness of the dual carriageway we approach the bright lights of the hospital. A technician on night duty hands over a specially sealed sample box, Nigel hands over a receipt, and the package is secured in one

➜

of the bike's panniers. Then we're off through the night again, west towards Birmingham.

6 Eventually, we arrive in a desolate car park, lit by the dim glow of a 24-hour Tesco. Standing in wait is Mike, another blood biker, one of Warwickshire's 'Freewheeler' volunteer group, identifiable by the fluorescent legend 'BLOOD' on the back of his bike. 'Nice bike you've got there,' says Nigel, as the package changes hands. We say goodbye and watch as the box of blood disappears on the next leg of its journey to the Birmingham lab.

7 Tonight, this nocturnal network of 25 regional groups of blood bikers is coordinated from the living room of volunteer Erica. Erica, described by the other motorcyclists as 'an angel', joined the blood bikers a little more than 3 years ago as a way of giving something back to the NHS after seeing the treatment her husband received following a stroke. 'I didn't want to leave my husband at night,' she explains, 'so being a controller was ideal. Controllers start duty at 7 p.m. and work till 7 a.m., and we work Christmas Day, Boxing Day, bank holidays and every weekend.' Erica also has a full-time job, as a sales consultant in a training company. She passed her motorbike test at the age of 50 and, some 13 years later, still takes her husband to hospital appointments on the back of her bike. She regularly tours Europe on holiday to see the motorbike racing, with her husband as pillion. 'It's a really nice way for us to get out and about together,' she explains.

8 The night begins and ends with the controller, who takes the first call from the hospital then rings one of the two or three riders on duty. 'I had four emergency calls last night. The last one was at 1.30 a.m.' The rider – who was on his second journey of the night – didn't get home until just before 5 a.m., when Erica finally got to sign off; controllers wait for a text from their riders to tell them they've made it home safely. 'I have bags under my eyes as big as Sainsbury's carriers this morning,' she laughs.

9 What draws the blood bikers together is a love of motorcycling and a desire to provide a service. But for now, Nigel and his colleagues have a low profile. We pull back into the garage of his home at 2.30 a.m. Doesn't he ever just want an early night? 'I never wanted to spend my retirement in my slippers!' he says. 'I love it – how much help we are I don't know. But I'm no hero – I don't have to be up early tomorrow. It's the people with full-time jobs that I really take my hat off to.'

10 After removing his riding gloves, Nigel reaches into his pocket for his phone. There's one more thing to do. 'I'm just going to text Erica – to tell her I've returned safely,' he says.

11 As for the blood sample he has been transporting, Nigel will never know what became of it. He has only once had an insight into the importance of his journey: a delivery to the Heart hospital in west London. Even that time, he says, 'I have no idea what they were for – but, when I pulled up, a theatre technician in his scrubs was waiting at reception to take the package.' Then he vanished back inside. Most of the time, vital though they are, the blood bikers are in the dark. 'I always think it would be nice to know the story behind what we're carrying,' Nigel says. 'We're really just the messengers.'

Questions

1 **Read paragraph 1.** Which two expressions used later in the paragraph continue the idea that the message is 'urgent'? **2**

2 **Read paragraph 2.** Using **your own words** as far as possible, explain:

a) **who** the blood bikers are **2**

b) **what** the blood bikers do **2**

c) **how** the writer suggests that their work is important. **2**

3 **Read paragraphs 3 and 4.** Using **your own words** as far as possible, explain:

a) the restrictions that the blood bikers must obey **2**

b) why these restrictions might seem surprising. **2**

4 **Read paragraph 5.** How does the writer create a contrast between the dual carriageway and the hospital? **2**

5 **Read paragraph 6.** Identify **one** example of the writer's word choice that makes the car park seem unappealing, and explain how this impression is created. **2**

6 **Read paragraph 7**, which is about Erica, the blood bikers' controller. Using **your own words**, explain:

a) **why** Erica joined the blood bikers **2**

b) **why** she chose to work as a controller rather than a biker. **2**

c) **how** the paragraph shows that controllers are very dedicated to their job **2**

d) **how** the paragraph shows that Erica is a keen biker. **2**

7 **Read paragraph 8.**

a) Using **your own words** as far as possible, explain how the writer makes it clear that Erica worked hard last night. **3**

b) Erica says, 'I have bags under my eyes as big as Sainsbury's carriers this morning'. Identify the figure of speech she uses, and explain what she means. **2**

8 **Read paragraph 9**. Using **your own words**, explain:

a) **what** 'draws the blood bikers together' **2**

b) **why** Nigel does not believe he is a 'hero'. **2**

9 **Read paragraph 11.**

a) Explain how the story Nigel tells in this paragraph illustrates the importance of his journey. **2**

b) The writer says that the blood bikers are usually 'in the dark'. This expression has two meanings. Explain how each of these meanings fits the passage. **2**

ANSWERS

Part One: Key Elements of Close Reading

Chapter One: Understanding Ideas and Details

Active learning, using own words, page 3

1 **a)** only be possible to see [rhinos, African elephants and leatherback turtles] in zoos

b) when he reaches his mid-thirties

c) nearly half

d) all kinds of birds

e) will have died out

2 **a)** 'Angus' has not been changed. Nor have the words 'rhinos', 'African elephants', 'leatherback turtles'.

b) You cannot put someone's name into different words. You cannot change animal names.

Active learning, using own words, page 5

1 **Gloss of** 'busy working mum' and **gloss of** 'wrapped up in modern life'

2 **Gloss of** 'the wonder of a sunset' and **gloss of** 'the decline in our birds'

Active learning, The Young Citizen's Passport, pages 5–6

1 **Gloss of** that readers will 'find the passport helpful'

2 **a)** They are trying to give a summary of the law.

b) Gloss of 'take further advice'

3 **a) Gloss of** 'using the law in the wrong ways can make matters worse.'

b) Gloss of 'Try to sort things out personally, if you can.'

Active learning, dolphin encounter, page 8

1 'a split second'

2 'usually sociable creatures found in their pod'

3 'confidently', 'cheekily'

4 'I had to do everything in my power'

5 'something I will probably never experience again'

Active learning, choosing a bank, page 10

1 How to choose a bank

2 Pupils should put each of the following ideas from the passage into their own words:
- Is the bank easy to access: is there a branch near where you live or work, and can you get access to your account outside opening hours by using online banking or a mobile app?
- Does the bank have a good network of cash machines so that you can easily withdraw money when you need it?
- Will they pay you a reasonable amount of interest on any money you save in your account?
- How much will the bank charge you for its services?
- Do they have any special offers aimed at customers your age?

Active learning, topic sentences, pages 12–13

Paragraph 1 – 1st sentence

Paragraph 2 – 1st sentence

Paragraph 3 – 1st sentence

Paragraph 4 – last sentence

Active learning, Bringing it all together, pages 14–16

1 'School lunches have many benefits.'

2 'If you are making packed lunches, try to keep them varied, nutritious and fresh.'

3 **Gloss of** 'far better shape mentally and physically' and **gloss of** 'get the most out of school'

4 **a)** 'If time is tight'

b) 'ideal'

5 **Gloss of** 'Getting your children to eat school lunches will save you time'
and/or of 'They are also healthy'
and/or of 'Homemade packed lunches rarely have such high nutritional value.'
and/or of 'If your children will be going straight from lessons to after school clubs and activities, it's good to know they ate well at lunchtime.'
and/or of 'Studies also show that at key times like starting in a new class or school, children prefer school lunches because they can be part of a group activity and make friends.'
and/or of 'These meals can even make children more adventurous.'

6 **Gloss of** 'you know what they're eating'
and of 'If you include food you know your child enjoys you'll avoid hungry days if there isn't anything on the school lunch menu he or she likes.'
and of 'Packed lunches can help you save money too'.
and of 'Bringing lunch from home also cuts out waiting.'

7 **Gloss of** 'Try carrot and cucumber sticks in a pot if your child gets bored with apples'
and of 'a thermos flask of soup or even pasta instead of sandwiches five days a week'

8 **a)** 'substantial', 'hearty'

b) So their body can digest the food (1) before bedtime (1).

9 'Pass it on'

Chapter Two: Analysing Language and Style

Active learning, monster poem, page 20

1 chomped, munched, gulped, scoffed, swallowed

Active learning, connotations, page 22

1 eating quickly/greedily/with bad manners/taking large mouthfuls
2 eating slowly/delicately/taking small bites
3 relaxed/not in a hurry/casual/no particular place to go
4 out for a deliberate walk/in the country/for exercise/energetic
5 angry/fast
6 untidy/careless/quick etc.
7 untidy/careless/quick/hard to read
8 gently/slowly etc.
9 quickly/firmly/strongly
10 deep/long sleep
11 light/short sleep
12 the smell is pleasant/beautiful/delicious
13 the smell is horrible
14 'obese' is more serious than 'overweight', suggests fatter/more unhealthy. Pupils may also identify 'obese' as a more medical term.
15 'gorgeous' is stronger than 'pretty'
16 'enormous' is bigger than 'large'

Active learning, My dog stole my tractor, pages 22–26

1 a) utility
b) just + really
2 a) spotted
b) cuts
c) quickly/lightly/easily
d) tend
3 a) quickly/suddenly/unsteadily/uneven movement
b) somehow
c) quickly/suddenly etc.
4 a) 'My stomach lurched' + 'My heart seemed to freeze'
b) quickly/energetically

5 **a)** out of breath
   b) quickly/suddenly/dropped away etc.
6 **a)** busy/lots of traffic
   b) loud/noisy
   c) fast/quickly
7 **a)** amazing/impossible/can't explain it etc.
   b) apparently
8 **a)** dimly
   b) tailback
9 slight
10 (extra) vigilant

Active learning, formal and informal language, pages 28–29

- Giving a close friend some advice about boyfriend problems **informal**
- Writing a letter to go with a job application **formal**
- Tagging a photo on someone's Facebook page **informal**
- Sending your dad a postcard from a school trip **informal**
- Explaining to the Head Teacher how you managed to break the staffroom window during lunchtime **formal**
- Opening your school's Christmas concert with a speech to welcome families, friends and invited guests **formal**
- Telling someone in your class on Monday morning what you did at the weekend **informal**
- Emailing a company's customer helpline to complain that a game you spent a lot of money on was damaged and would not play **formal**
- Writing an English essay about a text you have been studying in class **formal**
- Talking to a young pupil from your local primary school who seems a bit lost and upset **informal**

Formal	Informal
thank you	Hi Mum
a little girl	you're
that is unacceptable	I'm off
untrustworthy	she's like, really?
you are	thanks
drunk	dodgy
Dear Sir or Madam	that's no use
I am leaving now	blootered
she questioned this	a wee lassie

Active learning, jargon, page 30

Medical jargon

stent: a tiny tube placed inside an artery or vein

venflon: a small plastic tube inserted through the skin (usually the back of the hand) and into a vein

nil by mouth: the patient is not allowed to eat or drink anything

crash team: a group of doctors and other medical staff who resuscitate patients whose heart has stopped

ICU: intensive care unit

SCBU: special care baby unit

Snowboarding jargon

stoked: hugely excited and enthusiastic

shred: to carve or tear up the snow

gnar: terrain that is dangerous, and therefore also cool and exciting, to go snowboarding on

crunchy: a word used to describe something that is really great

squirrelly: loose, shaky or unbalanced

garage sale: a bad fall that makes loose items such as your helmet, goggles gloves, etc. land away from your body

Active learning, jargon, page 31

1 cookery

2 teaching

3 football

4 weather

5 law

6 mathematics

Active learning, similes, page 33

Objects	Simile
branches	like arms waving in the sky
ice	like sheets of glass
worms	like slow trains moving through the grass
ears	like saucers

- as cheeky as a monkey
- as brave as a lion
- as tall as a giraffe
- as blind as a bat

Active learning, metaphors, page 34

Mark on merit, based on the quality of pupils' explanations.

Active learning, The Sea, pages 34–35

1 Main metaphor is as line 1: 'The sea is a hungry dog'.

2 Accept any two of 'rolls on the beach', 'clashing teeth', 'shaggy jaws', 'gnaws', 'licking his greasy paws', 'bounds to his feet', 'snuffs and sniffs', 'shaking his wet sides over the cliffs', 'howls', 'lies on the sandy shores'.

3 Waves are crashing onto the beach, pulling or dragging at the stones on it.

Active learning, personification, page 36

Mark on merit, based on the quality of pupils' explanations.

Active learning, symbolism, pages 37–38

Mark on merit, based on the quality of pupils' explanations.

Active learning, Bringing it all together, pages 38–39

Para	Quotation	Clue	Type of image
1	'The boat moved with a nauseous, relentless rhythm'	Focus on the description of the word 'rhythm'	personification
1	'like someone chewing on a rotten tooth'	–	simile
1	'jaded, broken teeth'	'Jaded' means fed up and exhausted	personification
1	'The mailboat chugged its dogged way'	'Dogged' means determined	personification
2	'The mist flattened everything and sucked out all colour'	–	personification
2	'Trees became intricate, smoke-hued doilies'	–	metaphor
2	'they were grey paper'	–	metaphor
3	'The trees flung up their boughs'	Look at the trees	personification
3	'like drowning sailors'	–	simile

1 What feeling does the writer suggest by saying that the boat's rhythm is 'nauseous'?
about to be sick/unsettled stomach/makes passengers feel sick etc.

2 What is the writer trying to make us feel when she says the boat's movement is 'like someone chewing on a rotten tooth'?
pain/toothache/etc.

3 What is the writer suggesting about the boat by writing that it moved in a 'dogged' way?
determined/won't give up etc.

4 What is the writer suggesting about the trees when she says 'they were grey paper'?
delicate/flimsy/easily damaged/see-through etc.

5 What is the writer suggesting about the trees when she says they 'flung up their boughs like drowning sailors'?
panicking/nearly dead/giving up etc.

Active learning, Mary Had a Little Lamb, page 45

Mary had a little lamb	A
A lobster and some prunes	B
A piece of pie, a glass of milk	C
And then some macaroons.	B
It made the naughty waiters grin	D
To see her order so	E
And when they carried Mary out	F
Her face was white as snow.	E

Active learning, Bringing it all together, Task 2, The Bells, page 46

Rhyme scheme for verse 1

Line	Rhyme
Hear the sledges with the bells –	A
Silver bells!	A
What a world of merriment their melody foretells!	A
How they tinkle, tinkle, tinkle,	B
In the icy air of night!	C
While the stars that oversprinkle	B
All the heavens, seem to twinkle	B
With a crystalline delight;	C
Keeping time, time, time,	D
In a sort of Runic rhyme,	D
To the tintinnabulation that so musically wells	A
From the bells, bells, bells, bells,	A
Bells, bells, bells –	A
From the jingling and the tinkling of the bells.	A

Rhyme scheme for verse 2

Line	Rhyme
Hear the mellow wedding bells	A
Golden bells!	A
What a world of happiness their harmony foretells!	A
Through the balmy air of night	B
How they ring out their delight!	B
From the molten-golden notes,	C
And all in tune,	D
What a liquid ditty floats	C
To the turtle-dove that listens, while she gloats	C
On the moon!	D
Oh, from out the sounding cells,	A
What a gush of euphony voluminously wells!	A
How it swells!	A
How it dwells	A
On the Future! how it tells	A
Of the rapture that impels	A
To the swinging and the ringing	E
Of the bells, bells, bells,	A
Of the bells, bells, bells, bells,	A
Bells, bells, bells –	A
To the rhyming and the chiming of the bells!	A

Active learning, Task 3, page 46

Verse 1 alliteration: 'merriment their melody foretells', 'tinkle, tinkle, tinkle', 'time, time, time', 'Runic rhyme', 'bells, bells, bells'

Verse 1 onomatopoeia: 'tinkle', 'jingling'

Verse 2 alliteration: 'happiness their harmony', 'sounding cells' (alliteration of sound, though not of spelling)

Verse 2 onomatopoeia: 'gush'

Active learning, statements of fact and opinion, page 49

1	Teenagers are not good at getting out of bed in the morning.	**opinion**
2	Rats are horrible, disgusting, evil little rodents.	**opinion**
3	When it was released in 2015, *Star Wars: The Force Awakens* quickly became the most successful film ever made.	**fact**
4	Designer clothes and accessories are expensive.	**fact**
5	Scotland is a small country, with a population of about 5.5 million people.	**fact**
6	*The Force Awakens* is the best film in the Star Wars series because it has got the best female character.	**opinion**
7	Designer clothes and accessories are over-priced.	**opinion**
8	It is important for teenagers to get enough sleep as their brains and bodies are going through many rapid changes.	**fact**
9	Rats are rodents.	**fact**
10	Scotland is the best little country in the world.	**opinion**

Active learning, page 51

When I saw Ben on Saturday, he was sitting on the edge of the harbour with his feet over the water. I asked him what he was doing later.

'I don't know,' he said. 'What do you want to do**?**'

'Do you feel like going sailing**?**'

'Maybe,' he said, 'but aren't you worried about the weather forecast**?**'

I hadn't heard it, so I asked him what was making him nervous.

'Don't you know**?** They say there's going to be a storm this afternoon. Do you really want to be out at sea if that happens**?**'

Active learning, minor sentences, page 54

An empty room. A dusty old wooden trunk in the corner by the window. This must be the place.

Carefully, she lifted the lid. The hinges creaked. She pulled out the contents, item by item, laying them on the floor. Heaps of ancient cashmere sweaters with moth holes in them. Letters written on paper as thin as onion skins. Tickets for plays starring actors she had never heard of.

She found it at the very bottom. She could have missed it completely. It looked so ordinary. Just a blue envelope, with AIR MAIL on the corner. For some reason, she slipped her fingers inside, and felt the edges of a thin pile of sheets of paper. Bank notes.

Hardly able to breathe for excitement, she counted them. She counted again. Each note was worth a hundred pounds. There were ten notes. A thousand pounds.

Active learning, Bringing it all together, sentence types, pages 55–56

They stood at the top of the steep slope, peering at the river far below. Hannah could feel herself wobbling, as if something was pulling her downwards. Horrible. She shuddered.

'What should we do?' Jamie's words broke into her thoughts.

'I don't know.'

'We have to get away from those people.'

'Do you think I don't understand that?' Hannah snapped.

'Then do something!'

She looked at him, staring up at her. Her little brother. Wee Jamie, though not so wee now. It was her job to protect him.

Then she turned and looked back, over her shoulder.

What? A cloud? Mist rolling in?

No, it was smoke. Billowing, racing, choking smoke. And it was coming closer.

'Will you do something for me Jamie?'

She took hold of his hand as she said it. He hated holding her hand; he said ten was far too old for hand-holding. She didn't just take his hand, she gripped it.

'What do you want me to do?'

He hadn't seen the smoke yet.

'Run!'

Active learning, Bringing it all together, pages 58–59

Task 1

1	It rained hard all that day, and all next day too.	**3rd**
2	I've never been to New York, though I've wanted to go for years.	**1st**
3	You nearly ran me right off the road.	**2nd**
4	She had no idea how to do her Maths homework, and the revision for her Science test made no sense at all.	**3rd**
5	If you keep going all the way to the end of the street, and then cross at the traffic lights, you'll find the cinema just in front of you on the left.	**2nd**
6	I never drink milk, I hate eggs, and I'm not that fond of cheese either.	**1st**
7	The next time I go snowboarding, I'm going to take my own board instead of hiring one when I get there.	**1st**
8	You should check over what you have written before you hand it in, so that you can fix any little mistakes in spelling and punctuation.	**2nd**
9	He turned the phone over and over in his jacket pocket, willing it to ring.	**3rd**
10	The longest, hardest, most exciting day of my life actually started out quite normally.	**1st**
11	Those of you on the left side of the games hall can put bibs on and be the red team.	**2nd**
12	They were sitting in the front row of the cinema, passing the bag of popcorn back and forward along the row, when the fire alarm suddenly went off.	**3rd**

Task 2

A He's never been to New York, though he's wanted to go for years

B I had no idea how to do my Maths homework, and the revision for my Science test made no sense at all.

C She never drinks milk, she hates eggs, and she isn't that fond of cheese either.

D I turned the phone over and over in my jacket pocket, willing it to ring.

E The longest, hardest, most exciting day of her life actually started out quite normally.

Task 3

Mark on merit.

Part Two: Practice Assessments

The National 3-type tests

The first three practice tests, *Your Rights as a Shopper*, *Cream of the Crop* and *A Great Escape,* are designed to resemble the Reading tests for National 3 English, and are modelled on some of the tests in the Unit Assessment Support Packs (the UASPs).

SQA Unit Specifications say that, in order to pass National 3 English Reading, the candidate will understand, analyse and evaluate simple written texts by:

- 1.1 Identifying the main idea
- 1.2 Showing awareness of language choice

In order to pass National 3 Literacy Reading, the candidate will read and understand simple word-based texts by:

- 1.1 Selecting and using relevant information
- 1.2 Showing awareness of effectiveness

In the UASPs, teachers are reminded to use professional judgement and a holistic approach in deciding whether candidates have achieved the Assessment Standards. Candidates do not have to answer every question correctly as they could demonstrate achievement of the Assessment Standards across questions.

In all the practice tests, answers are suggested but not exhaustive. Other correct answers are possible, and all answers should be marked on merit.

Assessment 1 Your Rights as a Shopper, pages 61–62

1 a) *This article uses a lot of formal language. Give one example of a formal word or expression that the writer uses.*

Pupils should quote a formal word or expression.

b) *Why is it appropriate for the writer to use formal English in this article?*

Pupils should explain that the formal language suits the legal/serious/important subject matter.

2 '... *Read the section under the heading* ***be of saleable quality***'. *Tick to show if this rule applies to these situations:*

Situation	Must goods be of sale-able quality?
You buy something from a shop at full price	✓
The sales assistant tells you there is something wrong with the goods	
You buy something from a second-hand dealer	✓
You buy something in a shop's sale	✓
You inspect the item before you buy	

3 *Using **your own words** as much as possible, explain what it means if we say that something we buy is 'fit for purpose'.*

It works properly/does what it should do.

4 *What does the word 'privately' mean in the way that the passage uses it?*

Pupils should explain that the word means from an individual/from a person/not in a shop.

5 *Do you think this is a useful article? Tick one answer. Give a reason for your answer based on the text.*

No marks for choice of yes/no answer. Mark reason based on merit, looking for use of textual evidence.

Assessment 2 Cream of the Crop, pages 63–64

1 a) *Which word tells us the cans of Creamola Foam are very unusual?*

rare

b) *Which phrase suggests Roddy Nicoll has been keeping the cans hidden?*

tucked away

c) *The writer says that Roddy Nicoll 'claims' to have the last surviving cans of Creamola Foam. What does the word 'claims' suggest?*

he's not sure/can't prove it/there may be others

2 *If you were writing a factual report about Creamola Foam, give three details that you would include to help you explain this drink to someone who does not know about it.*

Many details are possible. Mark on merit, looking for facts about what this drink is/was.

3 *The writer says there was 'a frenzy of interest' from possible buyers. Give one piece of evidence to prove this.*

There were 43 bids/the price went up to £345/someone offered £900.

4 *Did you find this article interesting? Tick one answer. Give a reason for your answer based on the text.*

No marks for choice of yes/no answer. Mark reason based on merit, looking for use of textual evidence.

Assessment 3 A Great Escape, pages 65–66

1 *The passage names three hamsters who had dangerous adventures. Using* ***your own words*** *as much as possible, explain* ***briefly*** *what happened to:*

Pupils should use their own words as far as possible to briefly explain that **Lucky** was rescued from a bin lorry (**gloss of** 'municipal garbage truck').

Pupils should use their own words as far as possible to briefly explain that **Roly** fell out of a car and was found rolling his exercise ball along a motorway.

Pupils should use their own words as far as possible to briefly explain that **Mike** survived the destructive machines in a recycling centre.

2 *Quote the words or phrases from the passage which tell us:*

a) *that Mike was not badly injured.*

minor

b) *that hamsters are sometimes buried when they are not dead*

premature

c) *that you should not send a hamster through the post*

a highly illegal practice

3 a) *Why does the writer say that the 'rotating drum' in the recycling plant might have been 'familiar' to Mike the hamster?*

Pupils should explain that the drum is similar to a hamster exercise ball.

b) *Why is Mike the hamster now being looked after by Liam Bull?*

Pupils should explain that Mike's owners have not been traced **and/or** that Liam's father was involved in rescuing Mike.

4 *Did you think this was a good article or not? Explain your answer.*

No marks for choice of yes/no answer. Mark reason based on merit, looking for use of textual evidence.

The National 4-type tests

The remaining practice tests are designed to resemble the Reading tests for National 4 English, and are modelled on some of the tests in the Unit Assessment Support Packs (the UASPs).

SQA Unit Specifications say that, in order to pass National 4 English Reading, the candidate will understand, analyse and evaluate simple straightforward texts by:

- 1.1 Identifying the main idea and supporting details
- 1.2 Applying knowledge of language to explain meaning and effect

In order to pass National 4 Literacy Reading, the candidate will read and understand straightforward word-based texts by:

- 1.1 Selecting and using relevant information
- 1.2 Commenting on effectiveness

In the UASPs, teachers are reminded to use professional judgement and a holistic approach in deciding whether candidates have achieved the Assessment Standards. Candidates do not have to answer every question correctly as they could demonstrate achievement of the Assessment Standards across questions.

In all the practice tests, answers are suggested but not exhaustive. Other correct answers are possible, and all answers should be marked on merit.

Assessment 4 The Lure of the Bike, pages 67–69

This writer says that the bicycle 'has many downsides'. Using ***your own words*** *as much as possible, say what five of these 'downsides' are.*

1 **Gloss of** 'It won't shelter you from the elements'
and/or gloss of 'or protect you from the fury of your fellow traveller'
and/or gloss of 'It lacks the romance of a sailboat'
and/or gloss of 'or the simplicity of your own two feet'
and/or gloss of 'It will not give you the same sensation that sitting in £180,000-worth of overcharged horsepower does.'
and/or gloss of 'It is miserable in the wet.'
and/or gloss of 'No other form of transport ever takes it seriously. It is sliced up by cabs and menaced by buses.'
and/or gloss of 'It is loathed by motorists'
and/or gloss of 'and loved by the sort of politicians who would never dream of actually using it'
and/or gloss of 'It can't transport you from one end of the world to the other in time for Christmas.'
and/or gloss of 'It gets stolen, on average, every minute and a half.'
and/or gloss of 'It delivers you at the end of your journey covered in a light film of sweat and toxic diesel particulates.'
and/or gloss of 'It requires a lot of silly clothing.'
and/or gloss of 'And, of course, it is occasionally fatal.'

The above glosses may be very simple, e.g. an acceptable gloss of 'It will not give you the same sensation that sitting in £180,000-worth of overcharged horsepower does' might be 'It is not as exciting as a sports car.'

2 a) *The writer uses some negative word choice as she explains these downsides. Quote one negative word or expression that she uses.*

'won't'/'lacks'/'will not give'/'miserable'/'can't'/'toxic'/'fatal'

b) *Explain how the word or expression you quoted creates a negative impression.*

Mark on merit based on quality of explanation.

3 *The writer says that 'cycling obsesses people'. Using* ***your own words*** *as much as possible, give five of the signs that may show someone has become obsessed with cycling.*

Gloss of 'Cycling starts to become as much a way of life and a philosophy as it does a form of transport.'
and/or gloss of 'It spreads from work to weekends to holidays.'
and/or gloss of 'Cyclists nominate themselves for sponsored rides and charity marathons.'
and/or gloss of 'They stop thinking in miles and start thinking in kilometres.'
and/or gloss of 'Almost by mistake, they find themselves in possession of a whole fleet of bikes'
and/or gloss of 'They realise that one of the major advantages to cycling is the ability – more than that the need – to consume their own bodyweight in spag bol and chocolate cake every day.'
and/or gloss of 'They arrive at work early every day now, radiant with sweat and self-satisfaction.'
and/or gloss of 'At home, they talk about getting rid of the car.'

The above glosses may be very simple, e.g. an acceptable gloss of 'They realise that one of the major advantages to cycling is the ability – more than that the need – to consume their own bodyweight in spag bol and chocolate cake every day' might be 'They get to eat much more.'

4 a) *This paragraph contains a number of examples of exaggerated language. Quote one exaggerated word or expression that the writer uses.*
'(a whole) fleet'/'(the need to consume) their own bodyweight'.

b) *Explain how the word or expression you quoted creates an exaggerated impression.*
Mark on merit based on quality of explanation.

5 *The writer says that cycling has become a great 'success story'. Using* ***your own words*** *as much as possible, give two pieces of evidence that cycling is a big success.*

Gloss of 'its use in Britain has doubled and doubled again'
and/or gloss of 'Thousands now cycle to work'
and/or gloss of 'more take it up every day'
and/or gloss of 'It has allowed the reinvention of the British landscape, opening up miles of Forestry Commission land to mountain bikers.'
and/or gloss of 'It has connected people through events and races and just hanging out.'
and/or gloss of 'It has become the fastest and most reliable form of transport for people all over the country. In trial after trial, it is the bike which reaches its urban destination faster than the car, the bus, the tube or the pedestrian.'

The above glosses may be very simple, e.g. an acceptable gloss of 'It has become the fastest and most reliable form of transport for people all over the country. In trial after trial, it is the bike which reaches its urban destination faster than the car, the bus, the tube or the pedestrian' might be 'It is much faster than other ways of travelling.'

6 *This extract came from the opening of a book about cycling. Do you think it is a good introduction? Tick one answer. Give a reason for your answer, supported by evidence from the text.*

No marks for choice of yes/no answer. Mark reason based on merit, looking for use of textual evidence.

Assessment 5 The Drummer Boy, pages 70–73

1 *The first sentence says Edinburgh has many famous 'underground' legends. Quote three other words from this paragraph that continue the idea of things being 'underground'.*

tunnel, dungeons, passage

2 a) *Explain why the council sent a child, not an adult, down the tunnel.*

Gloss of 'the entrance wasn't large enough to allow exploration'

b) *Explain why this did not seem as cruel then as it might seem to us nowadays.*

Gloss of 'in those days, thousands of orphans were employed to climb inside chimneys and sweep them – so many Edinburgh children were used to crawling through small, dark spaces.'

c) *Explain why the council members gave the child a drum.*

Gloss of '(they could) monitor his progress'

3 a) *Quote two words from this paragraph that show it was difficult for the boy to move inside the tunnel.*

wriggled, wormed

b) *Which word makes us feel sympathy for the drummer boy?*

frantically/poor

c) *Which word makes us feel annoyed with the councilmen?*

safely

d) *What happened when the boy got to the Tron Church?*

The drumming stopped.

e) *What did this mean had happened to the drummer boy?*

Pupils are most likely to say that this suggests the boy was dead. Accept also that he had been attacked/that something terrible had happened to him.

4 *The paragraph starts with a number of questions. What is the effect of the writer using so many questions together?*

To suggest there is much we don't know, or similar.

5 *Does the writer make you believe that the story of the ghostly drummer boy is true? Tick one answer. Give a reason for your answer, based on evidence from the text.*

No marks for choice of yes/no answer. Mark reason based on merit, looking for use of textual evidence.

Assessment 6 Komodo Dragons, pages 74–76

1 *This paragraph contains a number of words that may be new or unusual for readers. Some of these words have been picked out in* ***red****. Find the right word in the paragraph to fit each of the meanings given below.*

a) *from a story or legend*

mythical

b) *careless and foolish*

reckless

c) *a guard or watcher*

sentinel

d) *amazed*

awed

e) *worked up or panicky*

agitated

2 *The writer says the airport has had 'a major upgrade'. Using* ***your own words*** *as far as possible, give* ***three*** *pieces of evidence that prove the airport has been upgraded.*

Gloss of 'used to handle 150,000 tourists a year; now it can accommodate 1.5 million'
and gloss of 'new terminal'
and gloss of 'lengthened runway'

The above glosses may be very simple, e.g. an acceptable gloss of 'used to handle 150,000 tourists a year; now it can accommodate 1.5 million' might be 'The airport handles lots more tourists.' As this is not a maths test, pupils are not obliged to say the number of tourists has increased tenfold.

3 *What does the writer's word choice of 'plummet' tell us about how rainforest destruction is affecting animals in Indonesia?*

Pupils should show awareness that 'plummet' suggests a sudden, major or dramatic drop in animal numbers.

4 *Using* ***your own words*** *as far as possible explain:*

a) *one benefit for the islanders of having Komodo dragons there.*

Gloss of '(locals like him) didn't have to move to Bali to find work'

b) *one problem faced by the islanders because the Komodo dragons live there.*

Gloss of '(a sudden) rise in inflation'
or gloss of '(number of people moving to Labuan Bajo) pushed up the cost of food and housing'
or gloss of '(demand for new infrastructure could) cut into the dragon's already limited habitat'

5 *Using* ***your own words*** *as far as possible, explain three ways that the government has tried to control the impact that tourists have on the park.*

Gloss of 'less than 10% of the national park is actually open to the public'
and gloss of 'entrance fees for foreigners were recently increased sharply'
and gloss of 'stopped the practice of feeding goats to dragons for tourist entertainment'

6 **a)** *Using* ***your own words*** *as far as possible, give three reasons why tourists might want to visit Flores.*

Gloss of 'several stunning volcanoes'
and/or gloss of 'rare birds'
and/or gloss of 'cave where scientists discovered *homo floresiensis*'
and/or gloss of 'some of the best diving and snorkelling on the planet'
and/or gloss of 'Komodo dragon is still the star attraction'

b) *The writer says that* homo floresiensis *or 'Flores man' is 'also known as the hobbit of Indonesia'. Why do you think it was given this nickname? Choose one answer.*

Pupils should choose answer iii: Because this person was very small.

c) *Explain why the last sentence is a good* **conclusion** *for this newspaper article.*

Pupils should comment on how it refers back to the idea of taking a selfie with a Komodo dragon, which came up at the start of the passage.

7 *Do you think this is an effective piece of* ***travel*** *writing? Give a reason for your answer, supported by evidence from the text.*

Pupils may find the passage effective as a piece of travel writing as it gives information about the airport, or because it gives details of other local attractions, or because it explains how much it costs to visit the park. Pupils may find the passage ineffective as a piece of travel writing on the grounds that it is more about wildlife than travel. Mark reasoning based on merit, looking at pupils' use of evidence from the text.

Assessment 7 NeverSeconds Blogger Nearly Silenced, pages 77–79

1 *Which technique has the writer used to make this headline memorable? Choose one.*
alliteration

2 *The writer says Martha Payne 'never expected her blog to spark a full-scale internet revolt'. Explain how we can tell from these paragraphs that Martha did not mean to cause trouble.*

Pupils should quote or refer to 'with permission from teachers' or 'as part of a writing project' and explain that the blog was part of her school work. Answers may therefore state, or imply, that the blog was somehow permitted or encouraged by teachers, or that it was her teachers' idea.

3 *Find* ***three expressions*** *in which the writer uses negative word choice to criticise the dinners served at Martha's school.*

Any three of 'measly'/'lonely'/'sprinkling'/'(a lot of) empty space'

4 *Using* ***your own words*** *as far as possible, give* ***two*** *pieces of evidence to prove that the blog soon had 'an impressive following'.*

Gloss of 'more than 2 million people'
and/or gloss of 'throughout the world'
and/or gloss of 'sending in their own pictures'
and/or gloss of 'Jamie Oliver (a veteran school food campaigner) sent a tweet'

5 a) *The writer does not approve of how Argyll and Bute Council acted. Quote one expression from this paragraph that shows the writer's disapproval.*

'ill-judged' or 'seriously underestimated'

b) *Explain how the word(s) you have quoted show the writer's attitude.*

Pupils should explain how their chosen expression shows the writer's disapproval.

6 *Using* ***your own words*** *as far as possible, give* ***three*** *pieces of evidence that Martha had a lot of support.*

Gloss of or reference to Jamie Oliver tweeting to her (to 'stay strong')
and/or gloss of or reference to 'urging his 2.3 million followers to re-post his message'
and/or gloss of or reference to 'became one of the top subjects discussed on the site worldwide'
and/or gloss of or reference to 'critics lined up'
and/or gloss of or reference to 'thousands signed a petition'
and/or gloss of or reference to 'supporters inundated council phonelines'
and/or gloss of or reference to 'pledged thousands of pounds'
and/or gloss of or reference to 'smashing her £7,000 target'
and/or gloss of or reference to 'from supporters all over the world'
and/or gloss of or reference to 'Donations … now stand at £61,519.07.'

7 *Do you think [the final paragraph of the article] is a good ending? Support your answer with evidence from the text.*

Pupils may find this to be a bad ending on the basis that it changes the subject, and discusses the charity rather than Martha and her blog.
Pupils may find this to be a good ending on the basis that it shows the impact that her blog had.
Mark on merit.

8 *Quote one expression from one of these paragraphs that shows that the writer was reporting on an up-to-date story when he wrote it. Explain why you chose the expression you have quoted.*

Pupils should quote '7 weeks ago' from paragraph 3 or 'last Thursday' from paragraph 8 or 'last night' from paragraph 14 and then show an understanding that these time phrases show the writer is telling a current story.

Assessment 8 What Milo Saw, pages 80–82

1 *Which expression shows that we have begun reading part of the way through a story? Explain how the expression you have quoted shows this.*

Pupils should quote 'A week later'. Mark explanation on merit.

2 *Using **your own words** as far as possible give evidence:*

a) *that Gran needs Milo*

Gloss of or reference to Gran needing Milo's help to get dressed

b) *that Mum needs Milo*

Gloss of or reference to Mum needing Milo to operate the satnav

3 *Explain three things that Milo knows about Gran but has not told to Mum. Use **your own words.***

Gloss of or reference to Gran leaving the tap running
and/or gloss of or reference to Gran coming into his room in the middle of the night
and/or gloss of or reference to Gran's belief that she is about to go on honeymoon
and/or gloss of or reference to Gran's belief that Great-Gramps is waiting for her
and/or gloss of or reference to 'she sometimes got the shakes so bad'

4 a) *What does the word 'snuck' tell us about the way Milo took hold of Gran's hand?*

Pupils should explain that this suggests he did it secretly/without Mum noticing.

b) *What does the word 'tremored' tell us about Gran?*

Pupils should explain that this suggests she is shaky/unsteady etc.

5 a) *Find an example of repetition used in this paragraph.*

grey

b) *What effect does the author create by repeating this word?*

Pupil should show awareness that it makes the surroundings seem dull/depressing/boring/dreary, etc.

6 *Using **your own words** as far as possible, explain what Milo's problem is.*

The simplest acceptable answer would be that Milo has eyesight problems/is losing his sight/going blind, etc. More able pupils or fuller answers will give more detail, e.g. that his vision is restricted/that he has tunnel vision/that the area he can see has shrunk/that he can only see out of part of his eye, etc.

Assessment 9 Arriving in Edinburgh, pages 83–85

1 a) *Quote* ***four*** *separate expressions Bill Bryson uses to praise Edinburgh.*

Any four of 'beautiful'/'beguiling'/'glorious'/'a happy experience'/ 'captivating'/'grandeur'

b) *Explain how we can tell from this sentence that the writer is not Scottish.*

Pupils should explain that Bryson speaks about the Scots as if he is not one, and may quote or refer to 'whatever it is Scots do'.

2 *Explain, using* ***your own words****:*

a) *one reason why the writer felt he* ***should not*** *have checked in to the Caledonian Hotel*

Gloss of 'rash' **or of** 'extravagant'

b) *one reason why the writer felt he* ***should*** *check in to the Caledonian Hotel*

Gloss of 'a terrific building' **or of** 'an Edinburgh institution'

3 *The writer says 'Edinburgh felt like a different country.' Using* ***your own words*** *as far as possible, list four things that made Edinburgh feel different.*

Gloss of 'the buildings were tall and thin'
and/or gloss of 'in an un-English fashion'
and/or gloss of 'the money was different'
and/or gloss of 'even the air and light felt different'
and/or gloss of 'every bookshop window was full of books about Scotland or by Scottish authors'
and/or gloss of 'the voices were different'

4 a) *Quote* ***two*** *separate expressions that show Bill Bryson did not spend long in the hotel room.*

Any two of 'dumped'/'immediately (returned to the streets)'/'eager to be out'

b) *Explain how* ***one*** *of the expressions that you have quoted shows us this.*

Mark explanation on merit, e.g. a pupil who has quoted 'dumped' may say that Bryson just threw his bags down quickly.

5 *The writer uses a number of different expressions to suggest different ways in which he walked around Edinburgh.*

a) *Quote* ***one*** *of the expressions he uses.*

Any one of 'trudged'/'shuffling'/'amble'/'picked my way'/'toddled'

b) *Explain what this word suggests about the way in which the writer was walking.*

Mark explanation on merit, e.g. a pupil who has quoted 'amble' may say that he was not in a hurry/had no worries, etc.

6 *Which genre of writing is this? Choose one: fiction OR non-fiction*

Pupils should identify the text as non-fiction. Mark reasoning based on merit, looking at pupils' use of evidence from the text.

7 *Does the text make you want to visit Edinburgh? Explain your answer by referring to details from the text.*

Pupils may or may not wish to visit Edinburgh. Mark reasoning based on merit, looking at pupils' use of evidence from the text.

Assessment 10 The Streak, pages 86–88

1 a) *Identify one technique the writer uses that makes her sound very certain about how The Streak began.*

Pupils should identify either word choice of 'sure' or use of short sentence(s) or repeated use of short sentences.

b) *The writer says that the 'reading marathon' she shared with her father began on a train journey. Quote the words from this paragraph that tell us The Streak had already begun before this journey.*

'he had been reading to me every night for as long as I could remember'

2 a) *The writer says her father will 'paint an entirely different picture'. What figure of speech is this? Choose one.*

metaphor

b) *The writer's father says he felt 'pleased as a peacock'. What figure of speech is this? Choose one.*

simile

c) *Quote the sentence which shows that her father thinks The Streak began before the night of the train journey.*

'I told her right away that we were on a streak, forty nights in!'

3 *Using **your own words**, give **three** reasons, why the writer and her father 'can never get this story straight'.*

Gloss of 'I was very young'
and/or gloss of 'he is getting older'
and/or gloss of 'some memories blend together with others'
and/or gloss of 'our individual versions … change so often'

4 *The writer says 'our rules were always clear and firm'. However, each rule is sometimes bent or broken. Using* ***your own words*** *as far as possible, say what the rules were, and how they could be broken.*

Rule 2: Gloss of 'It should come from whatever book we were reading at the time'
BUT: Gloss of 'if we were out of the house when midnight approached, anything from magazines to baseball programs would do'
Rule 3: Gloss of 'The reading should be done in person'
BUT: Gloss of 'over the phone would suffice'

5 a) *Give* ***two*** *reasons, using* ***your own words*** *as far as possible, why the writer and her father 'remember details from later in The Streak better'.*

Gloss of 'they are more recent'
and/or gloss of 'our record was becoming more impressive'
and/or gloss of 'became more nail-biting'

b) *By referring back to a detail from paragraph 5, explain what brought the reading Streak to an end.*

Pupils should demonstrate understanding that The Streak ended when the writer left home/went off to college.

6 *Do you think the writer has given you a clear explanation of what The Reading Streak was? Give a reason for your answer, using evidence from the text.*

Pupils who think the writer has given a clear explanation may, among other possible answers, suggest that the writer has explained how she thinks The Streak began/that she explains that they set themselves a goal/that she explains what the rules were/that she explains how the rules were followed in reality/that she tells us how long The Streak lasted/that she names some books they read together.
Pupils who think the writer has not given a clear explanation may, among other possible answers, suggest that the writer and her father are not in agreement about key details/that the writer seems to contradict herself about when The Streak began/that the rules are said to be firm but all seem to be flexible or easily broken/that the writer gives little detail about what they actually read/that she admits to not keeping track of what they read.

Assessment 11 The Mystery of the Clockwork Sparrow, pages 89–91

1 a) *Identify* ***one*** *detail the writer uses in paragraph 1 to make London sound unpleasant. Explain how the detail you have chosen creates this effect.*

Pupils should quote or refer to 'damp'/'steamy'/'last night's smoke' and suggest that London is unpleasant as it is noisy. Pupils may quote or refer to Sophie having to hang on tightly, and suggest that London is unpleasant as it is feels scary or unsafe. Pupils may quote or refer to Sophie standing between, or having to slip out between, other passengers and suggest that London is unpleasant as it is crowded.

b) *Identify* ***one*** *detail the writer uses in paragraph 1 or 2 to show that the story is set more than 100 years ago. Explain how the detail you have chosen creates this effect.*

Pupils may quote 'omnibus' and explain this as historical or old-fashioned vocabulary/word choice. Pupils may refer to the clerks wearing bowler hats as historical or old-fashioned clothing, or may make the same observation about Sophie's ensemble of hat, gloves and umbrella. Pupils may also identify the elderly lady's horror at a young lady like Sophie travelling alone as a historical or old-fashioned attitude.

2 *Explain how the writer creates a contrast between the Sinclair's building and Piccadilly.*

Pupils should identify both sides of the contrast: 'magnificent'/'white'/'immaculate' for Sinclair's versus 'smog'/'dirt' of Piccadilly.

3 a) *Using* ***your own words*** *explain* ***three*** *things Mr Edward Sinclair is renowned for.*

Gloss of 'elegance'
and/or gloss of 'single, perfect orchid he always wore in his buttonhole'
and/or gloss of 'ever-changing string of beautiful ladies'
and/or gloss of 'his wealth'

b) *Using* ***your own words*** *explain* ***two*** *ways that the writer makes Sinclair seem mysterious.*

Gloss of 'most of them had barely set eyes on him'
and/or gloss of 'rumour had it that he had run away to sea in his youth'
and/or gloss of 'there were already a great number of rumours about Edward Sinclair'

4 a) *Identify* ***one*** *technique the writer uses to suggest speed or busyness. Explain how the technique you have chosen creates this effect.*

Pupils should quote 'humming'/'activity'/'all about her'/'hurrying'/'whisked'/'hustled' '(in a) terrific rush'; **or** should refer to the writer's use of a list of actions; **or** should refer to the writer's use of 'or' to suggest many actions; **or** should refer to the writer's reference to a number of different characters. Mark explanation based on merit.

b) *Mr Cooper is said to be 'dressing down' one of the salesmen. What does this mean? Choose* ***one*** *answer.*

Pupils should choose answer ii: Mr Cooper is giving the salesman a telling off.

5 *The writer is trying to intrigue her readers and make them want to keep reading. Pick* ***one*** *detail we learn about Sophie in this paragraph and explain how it might make the audience read on.*

Pupils may **quote or refer to** 'Even a year ago, the thought of earning her own living would never have entered her imagination'.

or to 'she knew that Edith and the other girls would be only too quick to notice any shortcomings'
or to 'Once upon a time'
or to 'She didn't feel in the least like the girl she had been back then.'
or to 'Her face in the looking glass was familiar, but strange'
or to 'she looked older somehow, pale and tired and out of sorts'
Mark explanation based on merit: explanations need not be highly complex.

6 *The purpose of this text is to start off a much longer novel. Explain one way in which the writer shows that she is beginning a much longer story.*

Various responses are possible. Pupils may, for example, refer to the writer's use of details to set the scene; the introduction of the key setting of Sinclair's Department Store; the introduction of characters such as Sophie and Mr Sinclair; the hints that we will, during the novel, learn about what has caused the changes in Sophie's life etc. Mark reasoning based on merit, looking at pupils' use of evidence from the text.

Assessment 12 Blame My Brain, pages 92–94

1 *Explain, using* ***your own words*** *as far as possible:*

a) *what people* ***used to think*** *was the reason why teenagers could not get out of bed.*

Gl**oss of** 'just being lazy'/'laziness'
or **gloss of** 'choose to stay up too late'/'deliberately late nights'

b) *what people* ***now think*** *is the reason why teenagers are not good at getting out of bed.*

Gloss of 'special teenage brain (kicking in)'

2 *Identify **one** example of scientific word choice or jargon that the writer uses in this paragraph.*

Pupils should quote 'circadian (rhythms)'/'hypothalamus'/'biological'.

3 *Explain, using **your own words** as far as possible:*

a) *how adult brains behave during daylight.*

Gloss of 'the body clock is "on"'/'tend to be awake'/'difficult to sleep'

b) *how adult brains behave during the hours of darkness.*

Gloss of '(body clock) switches off'/'tend to feel sleepy'/'hard to stay awake'

c) *how teenage brains are different.*

Gloss of 'need around 9¼ hours sleep a night'

4 a) *Using **your own words**, explain **two** key sleep problems that teenagers experience.*

Pupils should, by using their own words, show their understanding that teenagers do not get enough hours' sleep, and also that they miss out on one particular kind of sleep, REM, or that they miss out on the sleep that helps them to remember, or to learn.

b) *The writer refers to someone called Mary Carskadon. Explain one way in which she makes Carskadon's information seem convincing.*

She describes Carskadon as an 'expert', or Carskadon refers to a number of statistics which seem exact/believable/reliable, etc.

5 a) *What technique does the writer repeatedly use here?*

rhetorical question

b) *What effect does she create by using this technique?*

This technique shows she understands what readers are thinking/gets the reader thinking.

6 *Using your own words as far as possible, find **three** things the writer says you **should** do, and **three** things she says you **should not** do 'to help yourself get the sleep you need'.*

Pupils' other 'dos' might be:

- deliberately be active at times when you feel sleepy
- catch up on lost sleep by going to bed early
- get lots of light during daytime
- sit in darkness in the evening

- spend time outside in daylight
- drink warm, milky drinks

Pupils' other 'don'ts' might be:

- don't let yourself fall asleep in daytime
- don't sleep late at weekends
- don't take drugs to help you sleep

Assessment 13 Made in Scotland, pages 96–99

1 *The writer mentions **three** important steps in the evolution of golf. Using **your own words**, say when each of these stages happened, and what happened at that point.*

around 1100: gloss of 'shepherds used sticks to hit pebbles into rabbit holes'
sixteenth century: gloss of 'different clubs being used to hit the balls into holes marked by flags'
1744: gloss of 'oldest surviving rules of golf were drafted'
1 mark for each well-glossed detail

2 *Using **your own words** as far as possible, explain why logarithms were important when they were first invented, and why they are still important to us now.*

When first invented:
gloss of 'seafarers could chart their position accurately'
and gloss of 'astronomers were able to calculate the orbits of planets'
Now:
gloss of 'laid the foundations for modern computing'
1 mark for each well-glossed detail

3 *Using **your own words** as far as possible, explain how we know that Watt's improvements to the engine made a significant difference.*

Mark explanation on merit, with a simpler answer getting 1 mark and more detailed or developed responses earning 2 marks. A simpler answer might be that Watt made the engine work much better (some sense of intensity would be required); more complex answers will gloss the ideas contained in 'increasing the engine's efficiency' and 'threefold'.

4 a) *The author says this was the 'first professional police force'. Quote an expression which continues the idea of this being the 'first' force and explain how it does so.*

1 mark for quotation of 'establishing'/'fledgling' + 1 mark for explanation

b) *Identify one duty carried out by the City of Glasgow Police that you find surprising, and explain why you are surprised by it.*

1 mark for identification of 'fire fighting'/'street sweeping'/'calling the time' as surprising duties for a police force + 1 mark for explanation of why this task may be thought surprising

5 a) *Explain in* ***your own words*** *what 'horrified' Simpson.*

Mark explanation on merit, with a simpler answer getting 1 mark and more detailed or developed responses earning 2 marks. More complex answers will gloss the ideas contained in both 'the sight of operations' and 'performed without anaesthetics'.

b) *Identify an expression which tells us that Simpson's discovery had a major impact, and explain how it does so.*

1 mark for identification of 'revolutionised' + 1 mark for explanation

6 *How does this particular invention not quite fit the title of the whole passage?*

Mark explanation on merit, with a simpler answer getting 1 mark and more detailed or developed responses earning 2 marks. A simpler answer might be that the phone was not invented in Scotland; more complex answers will gloss the ideas contained in 'Made in Scotland' and 'living in Canada'.

7 *What evidence is there that the first television was 'a primitive affair'?*

It was made of junk/spare parts/parts of other machines etc.
The picture was 'crude'/poor quality/only made of 30 lines etc.
1 mark for each separate detail

8 *The writer uses a number of expressions that tell us Scotland is often the first country to create something new. Identify* ***three*** *of these.*

'pioneering'/'ground-breaking'/'innovations'/'at the forefront'
1 mark for each, to a total of 3

Assessment 14 Message in a Bottle, pages 100–102

1 *Identify an expression that shows the writer's 'excitement' and explain how it does so.*

1 mark for identification of 'jolt'/'my hands were shaking'/'it was a miracle' + 1 mark for explanation

2 a) *Using* ***your own words****, give evidence that finding more bottles became an 'obsession' for the writer.*

Gloss of 'spending every spare cent'
and gloss of 'spending every spare moment'
1 mark for each

b) *Using* ***your own words****, explain why the writer believed he would be able to find more bottles.*

Gloss of 'had always beach-combed'
and/or gloss of 'when you figure out the knack of looking'
and/or gloss of 'you start finding more'

1 mark for each well-glossed detail, to a maximum of 2

3 a) *The Turks and Caicos are decribed as 'a flotsam magnet'. Identify the figure of speech used in this expression.*

metaphor

b) *Using* ***your own words****, list the evidence that shows these islands are indeed 'a flotsam magnet'.*

Gloss of 'bottles have been washing up on the islands since at least the 1800s'
and/or gloss of 'Museum features a large collection'
and/or gloss of 'I've picked up bottles from senders in the US, Canada, Britain, France, Germany, Spain, the Philippines, Puerto Rico and Switzerland'
and/or gloss of 'It's not just messages'
and/or gloss of 'I've found artwork, business cards, dollar bills … even a crumbling piece of wedding cake'

1 mark for each well-glossed detail, to a maximum of 4

Note that some good glosses may be very condensed.

4 *The writer says that the internet has made searching for senders 'easier'. Using* ***your own words*** *as far as possible, explain how the story he tells in this paragraph proves that this is true.*

Mark explanation on merit, with a simpler answer getting 1 mark and more detailed or developed responses earning 2 marks. A simpler answer might be that the internet helps him find people quickly; more complex answers will gloss the ideas contained in 'tried tracing her for 4 years' and 'within a day'.

5 a) *The writer says that meeting senders is indeed 'almost like going on a blind date'. Identify the figure of speech used in this expression.*

simile

b) *Using* ***your own words****, explain how meeting senders is indeed 'almost like going on a blind date'.*

Gloss of 'brought together entirely by chance'
and/or of 'no guarantees we'll have anything in common'
and/or of 'could be awkward'
and/or of 'excited to meet up'

1 mark for each well-glossed detail, to a maximum of 2

6 *In **your own words**, explain how the writer illustrates the idea:*

a) *that British people are 'especially welcoming'*

Mark explanation on merit, with a simpler answer getting 1 mark and more detailed or developed responses earning 2 marks. A simpler answer might be that a British sender invited him to stay; more complex answers will also mention that he was invited to Kent when the sender heard he was planning to visit Europe (i.e. extending the trip to wider area or new location), or that the bottle sender also spent time with him/took him for a walk.

b) *that he sometimes arrives 'too late'*

Mark explanation on merit, with a simpler answer getting 1 mark and more detailed or developed responses earning 2 marks. A simpler answer might be that he arrived after one sender had died; more complex answers will include that idea and will also explain the lengths to which he went to trace the sender, or will note that he arrived decades after/40 (or more) years after the bottle was sent.

7 *In **your own words**, explain:*

a) *what makes the first story 'funny'*

Mark explanation on merit, with a simpler answer getting 1 mark and more detailed or developed responses earning 2 marks. A simpler answer might be that the message was just from a teenager; more complex answers will show awareness of the difference between the apparent seriousness of the message, and the actual situation of a father–son trip.

b) *what makes the second story 'moving'*

Mark explanation on merit, with a simpler answer getting 1 mark and more detailed or developed responses earning 2 marks. A simpler answer might be that the message made the sender think about her divorce; more complex answers will show awareness that the message celebrated a marriage that did not in fact last, or that the message acted as a reminder of a happier time, or that the message showed her how wrong she had been, or how little she knew what would happen.

8 *Identify an expression that shows that the bottles the writer finds are important to him. Explain how the expression you have quoted creates this effect.*

1 mark for identification of 'can't see myself giving up'/'hooked'/'treasure' + 1 mark for explanation

Assessment 15 The Blood Bikers, pages 103–05

1 *Which **two** expressions used later in the paragraph continue the idea that the message is 'urgent'?*

'Right'/'downs the contents'/'grabs'

1 mark for each, to a maximum of 2

2 *Using **your own words** as far as possible, explain:*

a) ***who** the blood bikers are*

Gloss of 'men and women' **and/or of** 'all over Britain' **and/or of** 'who dedicate a few evenings a week' **and/or of** 'volunteers'

1 mark for each, to a maximum of 2

b) ***what** the blood bikers do*

Gloss of 'transporting hospital deliveries' **and/or of** 'stand-ins for the daytime professionals'

1 mark for each

c) ***how** the writer suggests that their work is important*

Gloss of 'responded to around 35,000' **and/or of** 'urgent requests' **and/or of** 'saving the NHS hundreds of thousands of pounds' **and/or of** 'They take everything'

1 mark for each, to a maximum of 2

3 *Using **your own words** as far as possible, explain:*

a) *the restrictions that the blood bikers must obey*

Gloss of 'have to stick scrupulously to the speed limit' **and of** 'stop at every red light'

1 mark for each

b) *why these restrictions might seem surprising*

Gloss of 'essential' **and/or of** 'without it, urgently needed medical supplies would far more often be stuck in traffic' **and/or of** 'despite the rush' **and/or of** 'they are provided with blue lights and sirens'

1 mark for each properly explained gloss, to a maximum of 2

4 *How does the writer create a contrast between the dual carriageway and the hospital?*

dual carriageway: 'darkness'
hospital: 'bright lights'

1 mark for each

5 *Identify* ***one*** *example of the writer's word choice that makes the car park seem unappealing, and explain how this impression is created.*

1 mark for identification of 'desolate'/'(lit by the) dim glow' + 1 mark for explanation

6 *Using* ***your own words****, explain:*

a) ***why*** *Erica joined the blood bikers*

Gloss of 'as a way of giving something back to the NHS' **and of** 'after seeing the treatment her husband received'

1 mark for each

b) ***why*** *she chose to work as a controller rather than a biker*

Pupils should give a **gloss of** 'didn't want to leave my husband at night' **and** should show understanding that being a controller allows her to work at home.

1 mark for each

c) ***how*** *the paragraph shows that controllers are very dedicated*

Gloss of 'start duty at 7 p.m. and work till 7 a.m.' **and/or of** 'Christmas Day, Boxing Day, bank holidays' **and/or of** 'every weekend' **and/or of** 'also has a full-time job'

1 mark for each properly explained gloss, to a maximum of 2

d) ***how*** *the paragraph shows that Erica is a keen biker*

Gloss of 'takes her husband to hospital appointments on the back of her bike' **and/or of** 'regularly tours Europe on holiday' **and/or of** 'to see the motorbike racing' **and/or** reference to her saying bike riding is 'a really nice way for us to get out and about together' **and/or** reference to her still riding a motorbike at age 63

1 mark for each, to a maximum of 2

7 a) *Using* ***your own words*** *as far as possible, explain how the writer makes it clear that Erica worked hard last night.*

Gloss of 'four emergency calls' **and/or of** 'last one was at 1.30 a.m.' **and/or** reference to her finally finishing at 5 a.m.

1 mark for each, to a maximum of 2

b) *Erica says, 'I have bags under my eyes as big as Sainsbury's carriers this morning'. Identify the figure of speech she uses, and explain what she means.*

1 mark for identification of metaphor + 1 mark for explanation that Erica means that she was, or looked, or felt, very tired

8 *Using* ***your own words****, explain:*

a) ***what*** *'draws the blood bikers together'*

Gloss of 'a love of motorcycling' **and of** 'desire to provide a service'

1 mark for each

b) ***why*** *Nigel does not believe he is a 'hero'*

Gloss of or reference to 'I love it' **and/or** to the idea that he is not being heroic as he does not have to get up for work the next day **and/or** to the idea that the blood bikers he admires are those with full-time jobs

1 mark for each, to a maximum of 2

9 a) *Explain how the story Nigel tells in this paragraph illustrates the importance of his journey.*

Pupils should show an understanding that if the waiting member of hospital staff was dressed in his scrubs, then the delivery was needed urgently/immediately or the member of staff had come from the operating theatre. Mark explanation on merit, with a simpler answer getting 1 mark and more detailed or developed responses earning 2 marks.

b) *The writer says that the blood bikers are usually 'in the dark'. This expression has two meanings. Explain how each of these meanings fits the passage.*

Blood bikers work at night (when it is dark).
Blood bikers do not know what happens to their deliveries.

1 mark for each

Acknowledgements

Every effort has been made to trace all copyright holders, but if any have been inadvertently overlooked the Publishers will be pleased to make the necessary arrangements at the first opportunity.

The Publishers would like to thank the following for permission to reproduce copyright material:

Literacy and English experiences and outcomes table on **page iv** reproduced by permission © Education Scotland, www.educationscotland.gov.uk

Pages 2 and 4 – from the letters page of *Nature's Home* (RSPB magazine, winter 2015 edition); **pages 5, 9–11** – *Young Citizen's Passport* (2013) by Tony Thorpe © Citizenship Foundation. Published by Hodder Education; **pages 7–8** RSPB, *Nature's Home*, winter 2015 © All Rights Reserved; **pages 12–13** extract from *Respectme*, Scotland's anti-bullying service, www.respectme.org.uk **pages 14–15** © www.supersavvyme.co.uk, by P&G; **pages, 23–24** © Guardian News & Media Ltd 2016; **pages 34–35** © James Reeves from *COMPLETE POEMS FOR CHILDREN* (Faber Finds). Reprinted by permission of the James Reeves Estate; **pages 38–39** First published 2015 by Macmillan Children's Books an imprint of Pan Macmillan, a division of Macmillan Publishers International Limited Text copyright © Frances Hardinge 2015; **page 47** The Bells by Edgar Allan Poe (public domain); **page 57** *Playing With The Boys* by Niamh McKevitt (2015), ISBN: 9781909534384 © Vision Sports Publishing; **page 61** – *Young Citizen's Passport* (2013) by Tony Thorpe © Citizenship Foundation. Published by Hodder Education; **page 63** © The Daily Record/Trinity Mirror; **page 65** © Guardian News & Media Ltd 2016; **page 67** Reprinted by permission of HarperCollins Publishers Ltd/A. M. Heath © 2012 Bella Bathurst; **pages 70–71** From *The Town Below the Ground* by Jan-Andrew Henderson, published by Mainstream, reprinted by permission of The Random House Group Ltd; **pages 74–75** © Guardian News & Media Ltd 2016; **pages 77–78** Victory for girl, 9, hounded by council bullies for putting grim school meals on internet' by Liz Hull. © Daily Mail; **pages 80–81** *What Milo Saw* by Virginia Macgregor, by permission © Little, Brown Book Group, an Hachette UK company; **pages 83–84** From *Notes from a Small Island* by Bill Bryson, published by Transworld, reprinted by permission of The Random House Group Ltd (and in the USA copyright © 1995 by Bill Bryson. Reprinted by permission of HarperCollins Publishers.); **pages 86–87** *The Reading Promise;3,218 nights of reading with my father* by Alica Ozma © Hodder & Stoughton, an Hachette UK company; **pages 89–90** From *The Mystery of the Clockwork Sparrow* by Katherine Woodfine. Text copyright © 2016 Katherine Woodfine, published by Egmont UK Ltd and used with permission; **pages 92–93** From *Blame My Brain – The Amazing Teenage Brain Revealed* (2007 edition) by Nicola Morgan, published by Walker Books, reproduced by permission Walker Books and Elizabeth Roy Literary Agency; **pages 96–87** reproduced by permission www.bbc.co.uk/iWonder; **pages 100–101** © Guardian News & Media Ltd 2016; **pages 103–104** © Guardian News & Media Ltd 2016

Unit specification information **page 119** and **page 122** reproduced by permission Copyright © Scottish Qualifications Authority.